Heydrich
Alan Wykes

Editor-in-Chief: Barrie Pitt
Editor: David Mason
Art Director: Sarah Kingham
Picture Editor: Robert Hunt
Consultant Art Editor: Denis Piper
Designer: David Allen
Illustration: John Batchelor
Photographic Research: Carina Dvorak
Cartographer: Richard Natkiel

Photographs for this book were especially selected from the following archives: US National Archives; Bundersarchiv, Koblenz; Alexander Bernfes, London; Staatsbibliothek, Berlin; Suddeutscher Verlag, Munich; Ullstein, GmbH, Berlin; Keystone, London and Paul Popper, London.

Copyright © 1973 Ballantine Books Inc.

First Printing: October 1973

Printed in United States of America

Ballantine Books Inc.
201 East 50th Street, New York, N.Y. 10022

Contents

6 Introduction

8 Assassination

16 Nemesis

34 Musician

44 Intrigue

58 Nazi

68 Power

96 Feud

110 War

140 Triumph

160 Bibliography

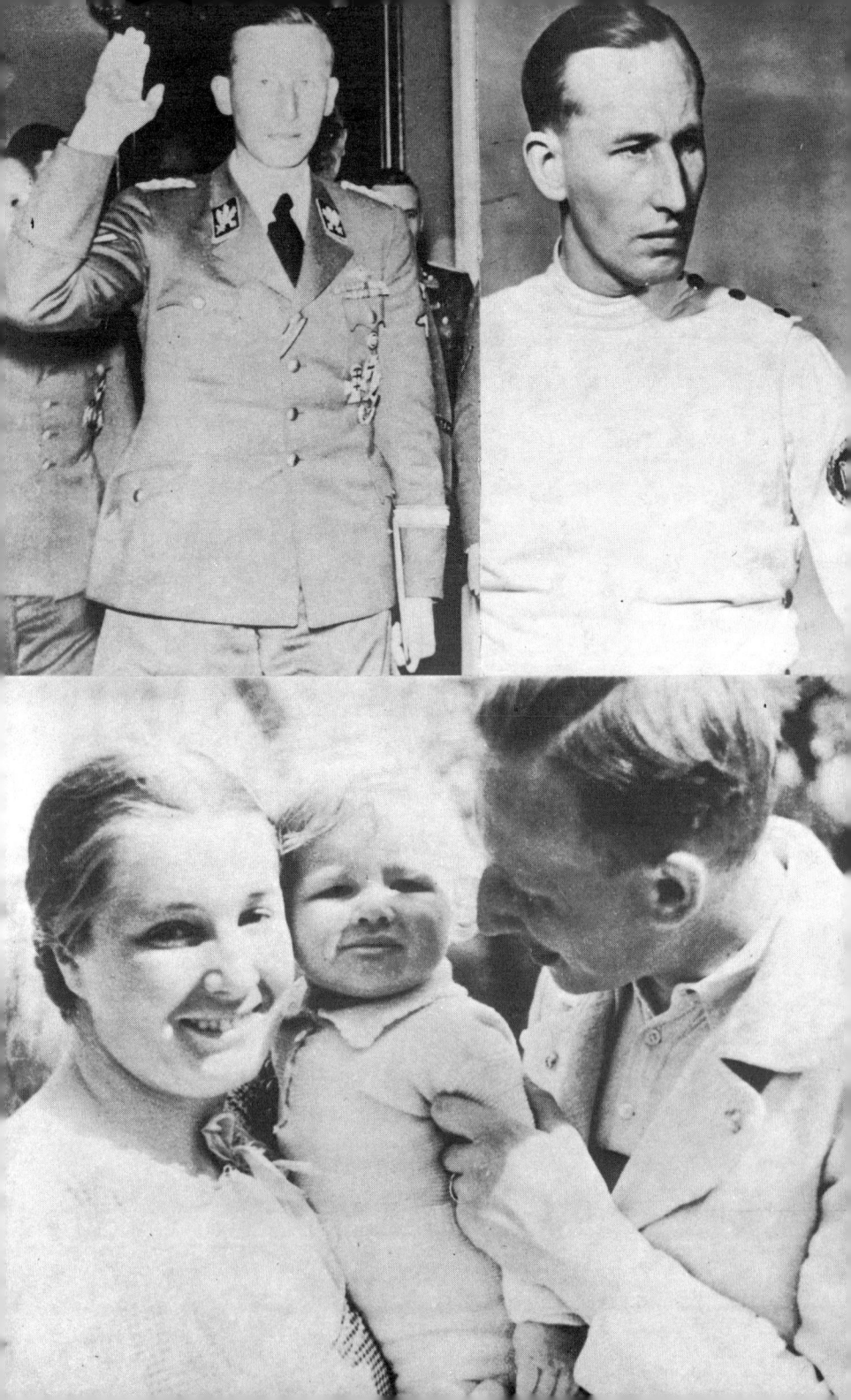

Himmler's right-hand man

Introduction by Roger Manvell

Reinhard Heydrich really arrived as an answer to Heinrich Himmler's prayer. To understand how he entered on his extraordinary and vicious career one has first of all to understand Himmler's oddly deficient nature. Himmler's very modest gifts, apart from a quiet pertinacity and a capacity to be always there when he was wanted, were best expressed in obsessive memoranda written at a desk. He was an organisation man, always bogged down by an over-careful attention to detail. However, from his youth he had dreamed of being a man of action dressed up in uniform and deploying men in the field, although his poor physique, his weak health, and his diffident nature, chronically incapable of making quick decisions in moments of crisis or emergency, meant that he was ill-equipped to be so. His ludicrous record as a general in the field during the last years of World War II reveal this. It brought comic relief to an otherwise grim story.

However, Himmler was an excellent, if over-pernickety organiser of the original SS formations, the so-called 'elite' guards who initially looked after the security of speakers at Nazi rallies and meetings. When he took over in 1929, there were less than 300 of them. He was, said Hitler later, to become the Ignatius Loyola of the Nazi movement. But what he most needed was an *alter ego*, a right-hand, or perhaps more properly a left-hand man to carry out in actual deed the more sinister work of the SS establishment once it had become the principal power behind Hitler's throne. He found that man in Heydrich, who joined him in 1932. Himmler made him, in effect, the second in command of his rapidly expending force.

Heydrich could have been a demonstration model for perfect Nazi manhood, which is more than could be said of either Hitler or Himmler. Himmler delighted in him, with his tall, fair, clear-eyed masculinity, and his hard, ruthless intelligence. He was an athlete and an expert fencer.

This was the real stuff, and he was, moreover, a violinist, which added culture to his other attainments. His prime weakness was lechery, but Himmler did not know, or did not care about this. Whereas Himmler was basically a puritan, a perverted idealist dedicated to making Nazism a pagan 'Order' with its roots in German mythology, Heydrich was an opportunist who laughed cynically at Himmler's obsessions behind his back. Once in the SS saddle, Heydrich grasped at every opportunity to advance his personal power and authority at his master's expense. However, there grew up an odd relationship between them, rather like that of an older and a younger brother. Himmler came to have a genuine affection for Heydrich.

This strange relationship flowered into an absolute dependence of the older man on the ruthless energy and efficiency of the younger. Although, quite naturally, Himmler would never acknowledge Heydrich to be his superior, he recognised their differences of temperament and came to fear Hitler's growing recognition of Heydrich's peculiar gifts when it came to carrying out anything radically unpleasant. Himmler's way round this was to allow Heydrich his head in administering the worst task the SS was to be given – the organisation of the genocide operation. It was to Heydrich in person that Göring, acting on Hitler's behalf, sent the notorious order, written in veiled language, demanding plans for the 'final solution' to the Jewish 'problem'. Heydrich's reward for undertaking this task was the position of Acting Reich Protector of Czechoslovakia, where he was to be assassinated. Himmler, while genuinely lamenting the loss of his ablest assistant, must have breathed a sigh of relief. Sudden death had removed the one man who might well have plotted to wrest control of the SS out of his hands, and would have had no compunction about doing so.

Assassination

Shortly before 9.30 on the morning of Wednesday 27th May 1942 the party arrived at the appointed place in the Prague suburb of Holesovice. They were four in number, though only two had been assigned to carry out the actual murder; one of the two carried the Sten gun intended to be the instrument of assassination, his companion being armed with a hand-grenade in case the bullets should for any reason fail to find their mark. No risk of failure could be entertained.

The assassins might be uncertain of the reasoning behind the order that came ostensibly from President Beneš, the exiled head of the Czechoslovak republic in London; but they were in no sense uncertain of their own fate should they fail to escape from the scene after the assassination.

The site had been chosen after much consideration and reconnaissance. It was a hairpin bend in the road leading down the valley of the Vltava from the village of Jungfern-Breschen to the bridge over the river in the middle of Prague. From Jungfern-Breschen to the city Council House was about twelve miles and regular observation had established that on a normal day the victim was in his office well before 10am and that his car turned the bend at about 9.40. The snag, of course, was that in the context of their observations there was no 'normal' day. The victim's ministerial life followed an irregular pattern. He spent nearly as much time in Berlin as in Prague, piloting his private plane between the two cities. There could be no certainty that on any specific day he would conform to a routine. The information assembled by the assassins' compatriots in the Resistance did not extend to knowledge of the victim's engagement book. The plan, therefore, left a great deal to the caprices of fortune.

But nothing else had been left to chance. The remaining two of the quartet were to take up positions 100 and 300 yards respectively up the hill toward Jungfern-Breschen and give warning of the car's approach by blowing the four dots of the Morse letter 'H' on whistles. (That they were Boy Scout whistles was, in the circumstances, not without a wry irony.) The terrain flanking the road was wooded and the trees were alive with birds. No attention would be aroused by the signal in the midst of so much warbling and trilling. It would be far safer than shouting or otherwise acting conspicuously.

Though most people were by this time in the morning at work the place was by no means deserted: housewives waited for the tram to take them down to the city; a platoon of German infantrymen was entering the woods evidently on some tactical exercise or other; a couple of turncocks concerned themselves with a seepage of water from a hydrant; one or two nursemaids perambulated their charges. There was also a steady flow of traffic, most of it military – staff cars of German officers, an occasional armoured vehicle, trucks with loads obscured by tarpaulins or bearing rigidly seated riflemen, a light tracked gun-carrier or two. And of course the trams, which screeched painfully as their bogies negotiated the hairpin bend where the tracks, conforming to

Reinhard Heydrich

Above: The Mercedes, badly damaged in the explosion. *Below:* The hairpin bend, scene of the assassination

as wide an arc as possible, were laid to within a few inches of the footpath.

At this point the two armed men stationed themselves. Their names were Jan Kubris and Josef Gabcík. They were both inconspicuously dressed in civilian clothes. Kubris carried the grenade in the poacher's pocket of his sports coat and Gabcík's raincoat was draped over the arm that embraced the Sten gun. They watched their colleagues walk up the hill, on opposite sides of the road, to take up their positions as warning outposts. Valcík, one hundred yards distant, remained visible as he stood at the roadside, Jemelík at the further station was lost to view.

It was then 9.35. With any luck the open Mercedes with the victim sitting beside his chauffeur should be approaching in a few minutes. Though they might have been any two harmless pedestrians waiting to cross the road, Gabcík and Kubris certainly had no wish to stand about on the corner too long and thereby perhaps draw attention to themselves. Like Macbeth on another occasion they wished the job done quickly. But a speedy issue was not to be their lot that morning. Studiously ignoring each other they paced a little, halted, paced again; gazed unconcernedly across the road, watched approaching trams as if awaiting one on a particular route, considered the traffic slowing for the bend. It was not so easy to be alert for a distant signal and at the same time appear to be alert for nothing but a chance to cross the road.

'After ten minutes', Gabcík was to record in their journal of events, 'we felt certain everyone was wondering what we were doing, hanging about. We separated and crossed the road a couple of times, then crossed back again. Then a policeman appeared and we took off in different directions, Jan up the hill and me down it. It would hardly have done for any questions to be asked; and I had a feeling the Sten wasn't all that well hidden by my coat. It was of course, but that's the sort of doubt that catches you when your apprehensive.'

Their apprehensions were to continue for some time yet. The policeman left the scene, continuing on his beat down the hill; but the time factor was proving more alarming. Was the victim not going to the Council House today? They had no knowledge of his activities since the previous morning. It was possible, even probable, that he was 200 miles away in Berlin. It was the great weakness of the plan that his movements were so unpredictable.

By ten o'clock there was still no sign of his approach. Nobody had challenged them but there was no suppressing their increasing uneasiness as the minutes dragged by. It seemed certain that there would have to be a postponement, which would certainly upset plans laid in London and perhaps even alter the course of the war. The dovetailing of schemes initiated by British Intelligence was of baffling complexity and no doubt the 'latest date for completion of order 27 May' was settled on for competent reasons. It would be bitterly frustrating for Kubris and Gabcík if their weeks of training at the spy and saboteur centres in Scotland and Surrey were to end in the feeble non-event to which the design seemed to be leading.

Such considerations were probably in the front of their minds as they began to wonder whether it would be possible to complete their task. Several times they strolled away and back again, more conscious each time of their conspicuousness.

'It'll seem a long wait, however short it is', their English instructor had told them impassively. (His codename, very suitably, was Icicle.) 'You know the critic George Jean Nathan's comment about *Parsifal*?' It seemed that they didn't. 'He remarked that *Parsifal* is an opera that begins at five-thirty. Three hours later you look at your watch and it's twenty to

six. You'll find the same seeming extension of time on this job.'

True enough. By ten-fifteen it seemed that they had been waiting for hours. But ten minutes later their frustration was ended. They heard, faintly, the four short whistles they were awaiting.

Immediately they were alert. Gabcík crossed the road and joined Kubris on the outer curve at the hairpin bend. They stood tensely side by side trying to convey an impression of indifference. A few minutes later they saw the dark green Mercedes approaching down the hill at speed. It slowed as Klein, the victim's chauffeur, changed gear to take the corner. Beside him sat the victim in the silver-trimmed black uniform of the SS. He was conveniently looking downward, apparently at some papers on his lap. Gabcík dropped the raincoat (it had been marked with misleading identification symbols) and aimed the Sten. But as if in connivance with enemy gods no stream of bullets sped from the short barrel when he pressed the trigger. He pressed again in panic and again the gun was silent. As Gabcík well knew, there was a routine to clear it when it jammed, but he could not remember it; the procedure had been driven from his mind by the sight of the victim suddenly looking up and becoming aware of the assassin's gun pointing directly at him from a distance of twenty yards, then drawing his revolver from its holster.

A confusing moment; and made the more so because Klein had automatically reacted to what was evidently a command from the victim to stop by slewing the car across the road in a skid. Simultaneously a tram that had been laboriously grinding up the hill swung round the bend and drew level with the assassins. Heads were turning at the sound of the car's skid; and another tram coming from the oppo-

Above: **President Eduard Benes.**
Below: Sniper position in Saint Cyril and Saint Matthew's Church Prague, where resistance fighters took refuge. The window and frame were riddled with machine gun bursts

Josef Gabcik **Jan Kubris**

site direction braked screeching to a standstill a couple of feet short of the Mercedes. But suddenly there was a sound more violent than any of these: Kubris had flung the grenade and it exploded against the near side of the car as the victim unsuccessfully tried to force open the door. Brandishing his revolver he vaulted over it, momentarily obscured by the cloud of smoke and dust caused by the grenade. He fired at Kubris and Gabcík, but they eluded him by scuttling between the now stationary trams. Klein had no gun but he too started off in pursuit, only to be recalled by a sudden shout from the victim, who was staggering now, his hand clutching at his side.

Passengers were now leaving the trams and gathering in groups with puzzled passers-by. No one had fully grasped what had happened. A collision between car and tram? An explosion? A shooting? There seemed to be indications of a chase, but of whom, and why? Also an injured man in SS uniform was now crouching in the road with blood forming in a pool beneath him....

This confusion lasted only a few minutes; but it was long enough for Gabcík and Kubris to escape from the scene and for Valcík and Jemelík to arrive upon it and mingle unnoticed with the gathering crowd. None of the four was under any misapprehension about the necessity of getting away before the police or military arrived. Inevitably everyone present would be detained for interrogation. Separately and as stealthily as possible they edged out of the crowd and away down the hill toward the city and possible escape.

Their departure passed virtually unnoticed because at that moment a woman stepped forward. She moved toward the victim. At the same time two policemen thrust their way through the crowd. 'It's the Protector' the woman said. 'An ambulance will be needed.'

Above: Heydrich and Karl Frank in Prague castle on the day Heydrich took over as protector. *Below:* Heydrich inspects SD Headquarters in Prague

Nemesis

The 'Protector' was less amiably known as The Butcher of Prague. His name was Reinhard Tristan Eugen Heydrich. In the confused few minutes since the explosion of the grenade against his car he may or may not have been recognized by the gathering crowd. His face was not publicized as was the face of Adolf Hitler, whose viceroy he was in the Protectorate of Bohemia-Moravia, as Czechoslovakia was now called; for though he was vain and arrogant he had too much contempt for the Czechoslovakian rabble whose affairs he administered to waste his vanity on them by displaying his face on every hoarding. They saw his picture when necessary in the newspapers, and if they saw him *vis-à-vis* they usually had good cause to remember him. He was not, in the propaganda sense, in competition with the Führer. He was not in fact in competition with anybody. He was Heydrich – a man unique.

He was also – though he would not have known that – a man mortally wounded. Splinters of metal from the wrecked car had pierced his back and side and lodged in his spleen. He was in great pain, and when a passing baker's delivery van was commandeered and commissioned as an ambulance and he was lifted into it to bleed among the loaves of black bread and tubs of fat he writhed and screamed. One of the policemen sat beside him on a sack of flour but remained indifferent to his agony. It was clear that he only wished to ensure that the Protector did not roll off the lorry; no compassion was involved. The same

Memorial day for war heroes, 1942.
Hitler talks with wounded veterans

policeman had been present in the cathedral square at Christmas when one hundred of his countrymen had been mown down by a machine-gunner while Heydrich and Himmler had watched from a decorative dais as if they were at a festival performance to celebrate the winter solstice. The dead had not been shot for anything in particular: the charge was the general one of 'subversive acts against the régime', and the theory behind their execution was that it would discourage others from making feeble gestures against the State. The policeman felt equally discouraged from making any compassionate gesture toward the Protector.

The unceremonious arrival at the Bulovka hospital of Hitler's viceroy in a baker's van quickly gave rise to a great uproar. The Medical Director, Dr Diek, telephoned Hradcany Castle, the official headquarters of the Protectorate, and asked to speak to Secretary of State Dr Karl Frank. That, he was told, would be quite impossible; Dr Frank never accepted calls except from officially listed correspondents.

'In that case', the Director said drily, 'he will miss the news that the Protector is in my hospital after an assassination attempt and that so far as my doctors can tell at the moment there is very little chance of his recovery.'

This revelation brought no immediate change of attitude: rather, a stiffening of it based on the assumption that the Director was either a madman or a conspirator in some plot. The Protector, he was told, was at this moment flying to Berlin. It became clear to Diek that at the other end signs were being made, or messages passed – no doubt to summon SS men to speed to the hospital and arrest the mischief maker whose mischief probably had some sinister purpose behind it.

'But it seemed that I at last convinced them', Dr Diek said later. 'I had with me the policeman who had accompanied Heydrich, and one of my own surgeons, Dietrich Hohlbaum, who had made a preliminary examination and was about to operate. Between us we succeeded in getting a line to Karl Frank. His response was immediate. He would, he said, get through at once to *Reichsführer-SS* Heinrich Himmler and tell him to inform Hitler, who was on the Russian front. Within ten minutes my hospital was surrounded by a squad of SS and patients of lesser importance were by their order bundled out of wards so that Heydrich could have a completely isolated room plus accommodation for Gestapo investigators.'

But no isolation or investigation could overcome the fact of Heydrich's mortal wounding. Lumps of wire, felt, leather, horsehair and glass had penetrated his back and side and lodged in the spleen and liver. The possibility of removing them was remote and the possibility of preventing the spread of infection nil.

'He would surely die', said Dr Diek, 'but that did not prevent Hitler summoning every physician and surgeon in his household, plus a number of specialists from other Axis countries, to probe and X-ray and advise. They could do nothing of course. Penicillin might have counteracted the blood poisoning; but such production as there was in 1942 was entirely in British and American hands. A nice irony. Heydrich died exactly a week after the attack.'

The assassins had a slightly longer life, for which they could thank the confusion at the scene of the attack. The knowledge that the victim was Heydrich had caused little but alarm among the onlookers – not for the Protector's safety but for their own. They saw the shadow of the most terrible reprisals threatening the whole city. It was as if with the departure of the ludicrous baker's van and the bleeding body of the Butcher of Prague they already heard the

The Führer in Poland

Heydrich and Frank take the parade on the day of Heydrich's appointment

firing squads cocking their machine guns in a repetition of the Christmas massacre in the cathedral square. The little knots of people broke up and, like the assassins, stealthily disappeared; passengers re-boarded the trams, and by the time the platoon of German infantrymen who had been on a fieldcraft exercise in the woods reached the scene they were baffled to find nothing but the wrecked Mercedes and Klein the chauffeur incoherently gabbling about the assassination of the Protector. The officer in charge could do little but report by field radio to his company office, which he did, only to be told to arrest everyone in sight and take them to police headquarters. But by then there was no-one in sight. There was nothing to do but await subsequent arrivals. These – men, women and children — were rounded up and put under arrest as they appeared. No questions were asked. They were simply told that they were for interrogation by the Gestapo. They huddled in the thin May sunlight against the railings that trimmed the corner, terrified and silent, waiting.

Karl Frank, who was head of the civil police as well as Secretary of State, was on the scene a few minutes after eleven o'clock. He was a toady of limited intelligence and extreme viciousness whose sinister appearance was in no way diminished by the fact of his having only one eye. Also, like Julius Streicher, the Jew-baiter of Nuremberg, he carried a whip, and this he now cracked as if bringing dogs to heel.

'The so-called Resistance', he said, 'will be struck from the face of Prague for this. All of you, and every single citizen of the Protectorate who was within reach of this spot this morning will be examined by the Gestapo and shot unless he can prove his non-complicity in the plot to murder the Protector and defy the law and order of the Greater German Reich and the authority of the Führer.'

That it was no empty threat they well knew. However innocent they were of complicity in whatever had been done the onus of proof was on them. Like those who had by chance been on the scene at the moment of the assassination and had in the confusion so hopefully melted away, they could already hear the voices of Gestapo interrogators and the lining up of the firing squads. They stared back at Frank with unrevealing faces; as little, or as much, as the flicker of an eyebrow might be construed as defiance. Four of the platoon of soldiers covered them with loaded carbines; the remainder had been sent to nearby houses to arrest the occupants and bring them to join the luckless assembly.

'There is no-one else', the officer in due course reported to Frank. He carried over his arm Gabčik's discarded raincoat.

'Then march them down to the Council House and keep them in arrest until I give further instructions. The *Reichsführer-SS* will no doubt have the Führer's orders by now.'

Hitler's orders, relayed from the Russian front through Himmler, were, when stripped of his characteristic ranting rage, brief and explicit: there was to be immediate extermination 'of the entire bunch'. (He meant the resistance movement.) And the prevention of the assassins' escape was not of greater importance than the 'stamping out of the entire canker at the heart of the Protectorate'. Himmler interpreted this as spreading the net of reprisal as widely as possible, on the principle that the more people there were exterminated the greater was the likelihood of netting the assassins with them. (It is on record, in the evidence of Karl Frank at his trial in 1946, that Himmler believed his deduction to be brilliant.) He ordered Frank to deal with the matter accordingly. 'And if Heydrich dies', he added, 'the scale of retribution is to be extended to the very limit that is possible without harming production for the war effort'. (The huge Skoda

The Nazis raze Lidice

armaments factories could ill afford to lose workers, however suspicious their background activities.)

Frank's first action was to have road blocks set up at every exit from the city and to stop all public transport. Only trains bringing urgently summoned reinforcements of SS from Brno, Berlin, Breslau and Krakow were allowed into Prague. He then declared a state of emergency and imposed martial law and a curfew. Every café, shop, restaurant and bar was closed until everybody in them had had their identity documents checked and been ordered to return home and await the visits of the Gestapo investigators. Soon after midday the radio and public address equipment announced that a reward of a million crowns would be paid to any person or organization giving information that resulted in the arrest of the assassins.

But the assassins were by that time implementing the first part of the plan for their getaway. They were to make their way to Resslova Street where, in the crypt of the Karl Barromaeus church, members of the Resistance were awaiting them with forged papers and a change of clothing that would turn them into bargees. Thence

The dead of Lidice

they were to travel downstream to where the Vltava joined the Elbe at Melnik. From then on their lives would be in their own hands.

In the event, however, though they reached the church without incident it was impossible to escape from it. Both entrance and exit to the crypt were concealed: the entrance under a movable cover which appeared to be the tomb of an ancient Bohemian warrior, the exit via stone steps leading up to what had once been a grating in Resslova Street but had now been replaced with thick glass pavement lights. Frank did not venture to close the church; it was Greek Orthodox and there were prevailing political reasons for not offending the clergy and congregation; but an SS guard was posted at its entrance during the afternoon and his sentry box was directly over the pavement lights. There was another way in to the crypt from the presbytery next door; and through this during the next few days the priests managed to smuggle eighty-four members of the Resistance. Until Heydrich died there was a frail hope that the worst of the reprisal measures might be called off temporarily to await the Protector's chosen brand of revenge; but after his death such hope vanished.

If, indeed, it had had much apparent justification before. Before the day of the assassination was over thousands of Czech hostages – according to General Walter Schellenberg's book *The Labyrinth* there were ten thousand of them – were rounded up and, on Himmler's personal order, a hundred of them were shot at nightfall without interrogation or trial, the choice of victims being made arbitrarily by Frank as he strode through the vaults of the Petschek Bank where many of them were incarcerated, his whip now and again being pointed at some man or woman he thought suitable for sacrifice.

The reprisals were by no means con-

centrated in Prague. It was Himmler's conviction that the Czech Resistance movement – of which, rather oddly, he had refused until now to acknowledge the existence – consisted entirely of Jewish intellectuals. A hundred and fifty-two men and women at large in Berlin and suspected by the Gestapo (on information supplied by Himmler's Race Relations bureau) of being both Jewish and intellectual were arrested and shot; and three thousand 'privileged' Jews – those who had had enough money to bribe the authorities to send them to the ghetto at Theresienstadt – were transferred to the 'experimental' camp at Dachau.

On 9th June, five days after Heydrich's death, on the basis of faked evidence contrived by Karl Frank, the most terrible revenge of all was taken. Frank submitted that the assassins had been trained in Britain and parachuted by a British plane into the village of Lidice, some twenty miles north-west of Prague, where they had been sheltered by the villagers. It was true that they had been trained in Britain and parachuted into Czechoslovakia; but they had never been near Lidice. (They had landed much farther over to the east, near the Polish border.) Lidice, however, was the chosen object of the Nazi revenge for the murder of Hitler's appointed viceroy. And there, on the night of 8th June, 500 special police from Heydrich's RHSA (the Reich Chief Security Office) were unloaded from troop transport vehicles. Their commander, Captain Max Rostock, ordered them first to surround the village. Then the living noose was tightened. Every house was visited, every occupant marched into the square in whatever condition he or she might be – clothed or naked, sick or well. Babies were wrenched from their mothers' arms and flung into the cattle trough to drown. Children were separated from their parents and beaten into insensibility if they cried or whimpered. Several women broke from the ranks into which they had

Reich Labour Service men level the sight of Lidice

been hustled and attempted to go to their children. They were shot dead as they moved. As the shift workers returned from the nearby Kladno mines they were rounded up with the rest in the square, their blackened faces and Cyclopean safety lamps giving them, in the merciless light of arc lamps that had been set up, the appearance of creatures from another world.

The small world of Lidice was sealed off that night. The men were driven like cattle into the barns and sheds and cellars of the farms and guards with machine-guns put upon them; the women were crowded into the classrooms and hall of the village school; the children, terrified into silence, were locked in the village hall. From the windows, from dawn on 9th June, they watched their fathers being brought in groups of ten from the barns and outhouses, lined up against the wall of a café, and shot. One hundred and eighty-nine were despatched in that way. The remaining men and youths, were, at the instance of Captain Rostock, who had become bored with firing parties, burnt alive in the barn of a farmer named Horak. All the women, save four who were pregnant, were taken to Ravensbrück concentration camp and put into the gas chambers. The four who were pregnant were sent to the Bulovka hospital where their babies were aborted before they themselves were removed to Ravensbrück to meet the same death. Of the children, seventeen who were less than five years old were sent to Berlin as subjects for the experiments of Himmler's 'racial experts'; the remainder were transported to Gneisenau concentration camp, where all but twelve died.

When all this had been done Captain Rostock and his regiment of murderers drove away. In the deserted village the walls and streets gave bloody testimony to the massacre that had been performed there; the young summer moon shone with ghostly light on the charred remnants of farmer Horak's barn and the blackened bones of those who had terribly perished in it.

Men so lacking even the most meagre shreds of humanity, so drenched in evil that the lives of others were to them nothing but the toys of monstrous sadism, are unlikely to have felt any spiritual haunting by the dead village. All the same, they, or their minions, returned with machines of devastation – with bulldozers, flame-throwers and dynamite – and ravaged every brick and stone, every inch of earth with a holocaust of ruin. In a few hours nothing was left of Lidice but a few acres of levelled ground scorched to destruction.

Every stage of the massacre and the razing of Lidice was photographed by cameramen of Goebbels's propaganda film units. 'It will be an excellent prophylactic', he said in his report to

Heydrich's memorial service

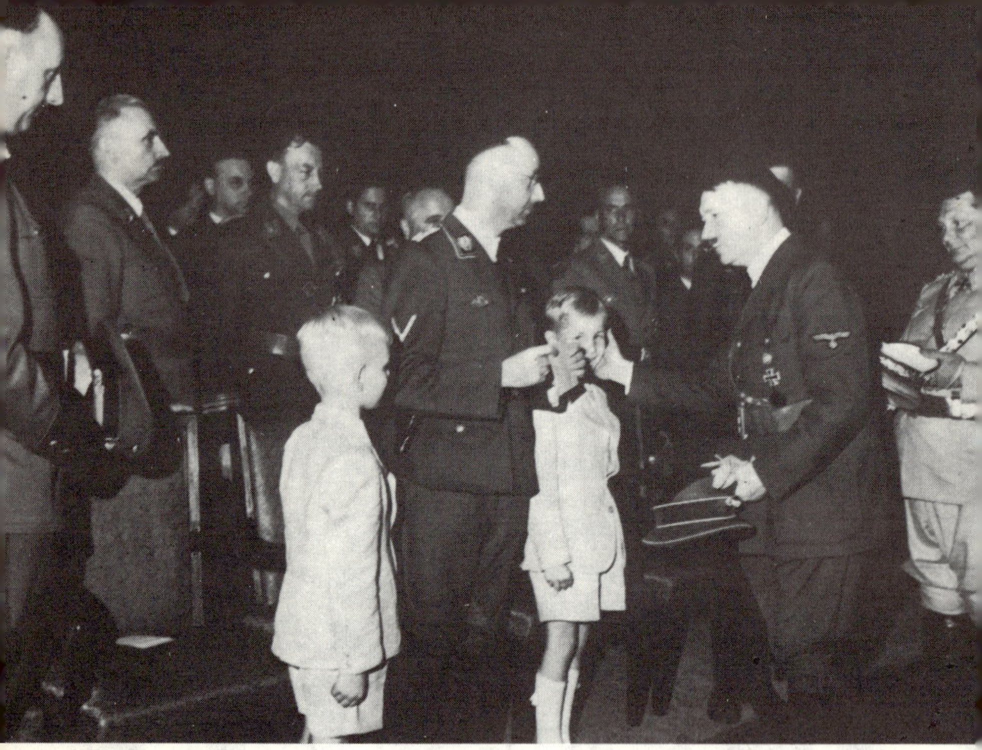

Above: Heydrich's children are handed into the care of Himmler
Below: Hitler comforts the bereaved

Hitler, 'against the future designs of Resistance movements.' One of those cameramen, Heinz Grath, recalls that there was a seminar for film men at which they were told of the value of their work and given medallions bearing the inscription *Rache* (Revenge) and a representation of Heydrich's profile superimposed on a representation of a holocaust. 'One would have supposed', he says, 'that it was a dignified and just revenge for an evil and long-planned plot against the régime, rather than the ruthless exterminaion of a village of innocent people'.

Nor were these the only victims of the demented cruelty of Nazi vengeance. Lezhaky, the village where the assassins had actually landed and been sheltered by members of the Resistance, was similarly razed to the ground after every one of its inhabitants had been murdered; Televaag in Norway was likewise disposed of after the villagers had been deported to labour camps on the Russian front; and in France the entire population of Oradour-sur-Glane, just outside Limoges, were burnt alive or shot to death by machine-guns as they tried to escape from their flaming houses. Such barbarous acts were always supposed to be justified by the discovery of plots or traitors or 'intellectuals' who had encouraged people to think for themselves; in fact they were no more than the manifestations of doctrinal insecurity. The monstrous balloon of Nazism must be shielded at all costs from the prickings, real or imagined, of its opponents.

As for those particular opponents, the assassins Kubris, Gabcík, Valcík and Jemelík – their fate must have penultimate place in this chapter of terrible nemesis.

They and the other members of the Resistance who had been smuggled into the crypt from the presbytery remained undetected for eight days. But it was inevitable that the reward of a million crowns would attract informers. These revealed that the priests of Karl Barromaeus had been in secret conclave with known enemies of the régime; therefore it might be worth while setting aside all considerations other than those of immediate necessity and initiating a few Gestapo arrests of the clergy. The arrests having been made and emphasized by the routine brainwashing and less subtle forms of interrogation, none of which had had the desired effect, it was decided to besiege the church and, as Frank said, 'tear it brick from brick if necessary' to establish whether or not there were enemies of the state lurking there. On 5th June a contingent of the SS division *Das Reich* surrounded the church and, after tearing down the altar, sledgehammering the walls of the side chapels, and committing various other acts of investigative destruction, came upon the false tomb. From that moment the 120 members of the Resistance who had found shelter there – including, of course, the assassins, though ironically it was never to be known for certain by the Secretary of State whether they had been there – were as good as dead. Fifteen minutes later they were in fact dead. Two machine-guns were lowered into the crypt and took their toll so deafeningly in the confined space that it was scarcely possible to hear the screams of the murdered.

The murdered Heydrich's screams of pain were to have a more ceremonious celebration than those of the Resistance victims, on whose shattered bodies petrol was poured and ignited. Later the same day, in the Mosaiksaal of the Reich Chancellory in Berlin, Hitler and Himmler both made funeral orations over the beflagged coffin of the Protector. Hitler's was, as usual, extremely turgid. It concluded:

'. . . he was one of the greatest of all Nazis, one of the greatest defenders of our greater German concept, one of the bitterest foes of the enemies of the Reich. With his own blood he has given us a pledge for the preservation and security of that concept. He was the man with the iron heart'.

Heydrich's body lies in state

Musician

Clearly Hitler did not mean to attach any perjorative sense to his 'iron heart' metaphor. He probably meant 'brave, ruthless, determined,' rather than 'cold' or 'implacably malevolent'. In English he would have chosen 'lion-hearted' or 'iron-willed'. Himmler also orated at the funeral; and leapt at the chance to indulge his addiction to symbolism. He forced a parallel between Heydrich's birthplace, Halle-on-Salle, and the iron in his heart by saying that 'he was born to the sound of the Halle foundry forging steel for swords and was imbued, as Siegfried was, with the mighty spirit of the forge'. Since the only works in Halle approximating to a foundry manufactured agricultural implements (including ploughshares, which would have pleased the prophet Isaiah), Himmler was somewhat astray. In any case, it was music that Heydrich was born to the sound of, not the beating of the hammer on the anvil. Specifically, his father wrote in a letter announcing the birth, to the sound of Beethoven's Opus 131 Quartet and Chopin's Fantaisie Impromptu, both of which are in C-sharp minor, a dark and stormy key.

'Four of my pupils were studying the Quartet in the big music room at the back and one of my best piano pupils, Irmgard Maelzel was playing in the first-floor studio.'

The elder Heydrich (his first name was Bruno) was a musician of some distinction who had had three operas and a symphony performed and was head of the Halle Conservatorium. Bruno's father, Karl, had been a

Freikorps volunteers

cabinet-maker employed by the Grotrian-Steinweg piano company in Brunswick; but he died young and his wife married again, this time a man called Robert Süss, who seems to have been rich enough to have had no occupation other than the management of his own small estate in Saxony.

Bruno Heydrich's wife Elizabeth was the daughter of another musician of minor fame, Professor Eugen Krantz, who directed the affairs of the Royal Conservatorium in Dresden and was adviser on musical matters to the King of Saxony. Eugen Krantz's wife's name had been Mautsch before she married; but of her – and indeed of all their forebears – more later. Some of them had significant influence on the development of the character and career of the musically born baby.

The baby's birthday was 7th March 1904 and he was baptized Reinhard Tristan Eugen on 12th April in St Moritzkirche by a priest whose name on the baptismal certificate is indecipherable but is of little account anyway. The point to remember is that Reinhard was born of Roman Catholic parents – though Bruno had been a Lutheran who had changed his religion on marrying Elizabeth Krautz – and was baptized into the Roman faith. This fact will later be seen to be a puzzling one, and not without its own importance.

It is not puzzling that he inherited and quickly displayed considerable musical talent. His mother also was a musician of great ability. She taught both voice and piano at the Conservatorium and gave many *lieder* recitals in Halle and other Saxon towns. Reinhard was able to read music at the age of five and to take part in school concerts as a violinist at seven. He became a pupil of the organist of the Lutheran cathedral (Handel had been organist there) and was a competent performer on several brass and woodwind instruments.

The spectrum of his ordinary academic achievements was no less broad: his work in history, literature, philo-

Freikorps leaders gather in Munich

sophy and those other studies collectively known as the Humanities was outstanding. He also became a good all-round sportsman: swimming, tennis, fencing, riding, and sailing all being accomplishments in which his record was excellent. Unlike Hitler, who had a crippled mind, or Goebbels, who had a crippled foot and a bitterly malevolent nature, or Himmler, who was a cringing sycophant, or Göring, who was a conceited bully – and all of whom showed early signs of these unpleasing traits – Reinhard Heydrich the boy and youth displayed all the characteristics of what used to be known in England as 'the good public-school type', destined for the Diplomatic Service, the Church, the Navy or the Army. He was tall, blond, slender and, on the face of it so to speak, handsome. But as he passed from boyhood to youth it could be discerned that his good looks were marred: his lips were too full and straight, his eyes rather too small and too close together. All the same, such a talented and superficially personable young man naturally became very popular, though the depth of his friendships might be questioned. Better, perhaps, to say that he had innumerable lighthearted acquaintances – all of whom tempered their amity with a certain amount of reserve. They might have denied it; but one of them, Klaus Schmidt, says that there was a definite feeling 'that you couldn't approach too near, that he felt himself in some way superior to you'. A carapace developed to protect a certain hidden shyness or insecurity perhaps. That would be the charitable view.

It was naturally assumed that with his considerable musical talents and family background he would make music his career. But as with tens of thousands of other young men in the second decade of the 20th century the war set the points for a different track.

His intended *alma mater*, Bonn, where it had been planned that he should graduate as a Doctor of Music, never saw him. Another activity had gained his devotion by the time he passed out of the Halle *Reformgymnasium* (High School) at the end of the Easter semester 1922: soldiering. He had joined the Halle company of the *Friekorps* in 1920, when it was little more than an offshoot of the German equivalent of the Officers' Training Corps. The way into it was by achievement in sport and an actively resentful attitude toward the Versailles Treaty and the Weimar Republic. Fencing was of course the sport that had most prestige in the defeated and abdicated Kaiser's empire of Hohenzollern tradition, and Heydrich was a brilliant performer in the art. Its practice took him weekly to the Halle drill hall where the local company of the humiliated remnants of the German army met. Only 100,000 officers and men were permitted by the terms of the V rsailles Treaty as Germany's

President Ebert with Secretary of State Meissner, May Day 1919

entire standing army; and the resentment felt by these handfuls of scorned representatives of Prussian militaristic tradition was bound to be exacerbated by the increasingly frequent presence of unemployed ex-officers who had welded themselves into secretly armed opponents of the Republic calling themselves *Freikorps*. They were, they said, 'free of all but dedication to return Germany to its former national glory and to dislodge the President, Friedrich Ebert, from his pinnacle of shame as the collaborator with the forces of defe

All of which sounded very noble and dignified. But there was little nobility and less dignity about the *Freikorps'* methods. They brawled in the streets and beer cellars, seized and raped the wives and daughters of Republicans and Left-wingers, held kangaroo court 'trials' of suspected sympathizers of Ebert and Chancellor Scheidemann, and in general portrayed all the embryonic signs of the organization of thugs they were later to become.

Such behaviour had what might be thought of as an improbable attraction for the meritoriously educated Heydrich· but in fact, as will be seen,

Chancellor Scheidemann

it was completely in character. Beneath the glaze of the Humanities was an icy inhumanity that revelled in violence and the more eclectic forms of thuggery. The euphemism 'youthful high spirits' can, however, do much to account for the more obvious deviations from honourable dedication to an allegedly just cause. Heydrich was several times in trouble with the civil police over such matters as the breaking of Republican sympathizers' windows and the daubing of their front doors with the word 'traitor'. (An anticipatory glimpse of the yellow Star of David and the expletive 'Jew' that in a few years would become universally daubed through Hitler's Reich.) But the police and magistracy were feeble and corrupt; the Heydrichs were extremely respectable; the blind eye was turned and the mild reprimand served all the purposes of punishment. It was understood that young Heydrich was 'having his fling' before settling down to the career of a professional musician.

The other cliché, 'sowing his wild oats', was also understood with appropriate nods and winks. What burgeoning German girl could resist the archetypal Siegfried? Not many did, seemingly. Heydrich was later described by Walter Schellenberg, the Nazi spy, as the ravisher of every virgin in Berlin except one – that one being the angel on top of the victory column, which was too high for him to reach; and one of the professors at the *Reformgymnasium,* seeing him doodling libidinous drawings while sitting for an examination observed that he was 'supposed to be dealing with semantics, not sementics'.

One day in the summer of 1921 he was introduced by his fellow student Klaus Schmidt to a girl called Rosa Stapel, whom he amorously pursued – with what object can scarcely be doubted – for a brief spell. No doubt Rosa fell victim to his charm and good looks; there is little evidence on the subject; and the association would not be worth noting save for one reason: through it he met a friend of Rosa's brother Ernst, a young naval cadet called Rainer Thiess. Thiess too would be unimportant if he had not formed a further link in the chain that was soon to bind Heydrich to a career very different from music.

The German navy was virtually non-existent as a battle force; anyway in theory. But the terms of the Versailles treaty permitted volunteers to train aboard disarmed vessels, one of which was the cruiser *Berlin*, docked at Kiel, and to that ship Thiess had been posted. Kiel was also his home and he invited Heydrich there in August 1922. 'I told him to bring his violin because my sister often joined Frau Canaris for chamber music on Sunday evenings and I thought she might welcome a bit of new talent'. Thus Rainer Thiess, reported in an article, *Wehrmacht und Partei,* by Admiral Wilhelm Canaris, published in 1936. In 1922 Canaris was principal executive officer aboard the *Berlin* and held the rank of commander; but that appointment was only a necessary mask for his activities as a spy and an organizer of Germany's secret rearmament programme. He had been married for three years to Erika Waag, who had been one of Eugen Krantz's pupils at the Dresden Royal Conservatorium and remembered Heydrich's mother, Elizabeth, as a young fellow pupil. Erika Canaris was a cellist of considerable accomplishment and a dedicated organizer of chamber concerts for devotees of Haydn and Mozart, so she welcomed the promising talent of a new violinist who might enable her to increase the number of her *Kammermusik* occasions. Heydrich stayed in Kiel for three weeks instead of the weekend that had been planned and at the end of that time had, according to Canaris, 'seen the overwhelming need to take an active part in restoring the Kaiser and Germany's greatness'.

The training ship *Berlin*

Admiral Canaris with his officers aboard the *Schlesien*

What Heydrich had in fact seen was the greatest opportunity for self-advancement that had yet presented itself. The intrigues that had briefly revealed themselves through Canaris's conversations engrossed him. They were intrigues that suggested power – secret, latent power that could be manipulated. 'Commander Canaris', he wrote to his father, 'has entirely convinced me that the navy is the life for me. I see possibilities there that would never exist in music. The world of music is a world in which everyone is subservient to the wishes of the composer and the audience. I do not wish to be subservient. Least of all do I wish to be a subservient musician in a subservient Germany.'

There was evidently a reproachful reply from Bruno Heydrich, for a second letter from Kiel, dated 3rd September 1922, attempts some amends.

'Of course I will do as you ask. I have no wish to grieve you or Mother. But it is clear to me that any further thought on the matter will be unprofitable. All the same I will, as you suggest, seek Divine guidance.'

It is highly improbable that he did anything of the sort. According to Klaus Schmidt he was 'in the midst of a massive atheistic period such as

many students go through, questioning everything and finding all the old truths hollow. But in his case, as I see it now, it was really a virulent anti-Catholicism that was afflicting him. He was reading a lot of anti-Popish stuff and studying racialist theories. His promise to seek Divine Guidance was intended in mockery.'

At all events he volunteered as a naval cadet and was accepted. Bruno Heydrich seems to have accepted the decision philosophically. He had never been happy about his son's membership of the *Freikorps*, which he saw as a dangerous organization pursuing a policy of shockingly inflammatory activities. The navy, pitifully restricted though it was, still embraced the honourable German traditions and offered a disciplined life for a young man. 'Your mother and I regret your withdrawal from the career in which you have shown so much talent; but no doubt everything is for the best.'

The elder Heydrich may be forgiven for his Panglossian philosophy: he was a conventional man with a conventional faith in the turns of fortune. But for vast numbers of people his son's secession from the vocation of music proved to be a disastrous turning point.

Intrigue

It was, however, music that provided the façade for his continued visits to the Canaris home. A naval cadet undergoing ordinary instructional duties has no excuse for social intercourse with his commanding officer; indeed all disciplinary conventions argue against such an association. But it is retrospectively clear that Canaris for one reason or another recognized in Heydrich a potential conspirator in the surreptitious affairs in which he himself was engaged. And Erika's musical soirées provided all that was necessary in the way of cover.

As to the clandestine affairs in which Canaris was engaged, some indication is needed of his character and earlier activities – not easy to provide, since the business of spies, secret agents, and behind-the-scenes string-pullers naturally is to ensure their own elusiveness, so that it soon becomes difficult to find the way out of the maze of double-crossings and to separate clues from red herrings. But to stretch the facts we have to their limit we know that:

He came from Dortmund, where he was born in 1887. Like Himmler, he was pettily inquisitive – not in the normal childish way of seeking information to satisfy curiosity, but rather for mercenary reasons. He would collect and sell information to those who needed it and were willing to pay. Schoolboys seeking cribs, lovers needing solitude, embryo blackmailers amassing knowledge, bullies awaiting victims, thieves wanting sentries to call *cave* – there was a ready market for the snooper's wares and Canaris soon acquired the nickname *Kieker*, meaning Peeping Tom. In the Imperial Naval Academy at Kiel, which he entered as a cadet in 1905, his talents as an informer and quidnunc were referred to rather more politely as 'the keenest powers of observation and diplomacy'. The youth who was to become the head of Hitler's *Abwehr*, the High Command Intelligence Service, quickly had his abilities recognized.

Many of those abilities were more conventionally laudable than snooping. He was a man of considerable physical daring and *sang froid*. Aboard the cruiser *Dresden* as a lieutenant in 1914 he displayed both bravery and endurance when his ship grounded on a reef during the battle of the Falkland Islands. Challenges of all kinds amused and exhilarated him. Interned in a prison camp on an island off the coast of Chile near Valparaiso, he escaped by stealing, first, a fisherman's boat to row to the mainland in, then the horse belonging to the police chief of Valparaiso, on which he crossed the Andes without pursuit (so cunningly had he covered his tracks), arriving two months later in Buenos Aires complete with a new identity as a Chilean business man named Reed Rosas. He persuaded the Chilean consul of the urgent necessity of securing a passage to Rotterdam, where relatives of his dead mother were, he said, anxiously awaiting him so that a huge inheritance could be properly divided. The history of human credulousness shows that very often the tallest stories have been believed by the greatest sceptics. With money and a false passport in his pocket Canaris shipped on the Dutch passenger liner *Frisia* and arrived in

Admiral Canaris and Heydrich at dinner

Rotterdam speaking fluent Spanish and seeking suppliers of railway engines for a new government-financed railway in Chile. By this device he passed through all control posts in neutral Holland and went straight to Berlin to report.

Clearly any man with as much *nous* as Canaris had displayed was a candidate for the improvement of the Intelligence service (which in Germany in the First World War was abysmally bad, lacking, as it did, both competent direction and personnel). It was not long before he was sent to Madrid as a full-time spy feeding back information about the staff of the German Embassy there, some of whom were suspected – and rightly – of leaking information about German troop movements to British agents.

For a couple of years he pursued this undercover activity then asked to return to naval duties. On his way back to Germany via Italy in a U-boat he was arrested at the Italian-Swiss border on suspicion of spying activities by the Italian police and imprisoned in Genoa. Conveniently, a priest was sent to see to his spiritual welfare (Canaris was a Lutheran and therefore, in Italian eyes, greatly in need of conversion) and reaped an inequitable reward for his concern, for Canaris seized and strangled him and stole his clothes to escape in.

Shoals of red herrings obscure his undercover ploys during the rest of the Kaiser's war. On the face of things he had ordinary naval appointments,

Above: Karl Liebknacht. *Right:* Rosa Luxemburg—both murdered.

commands and ranks. But from time to time one comes across glimpses of curious missions: scraps of conversations with, for example, Sir Roger Casement; references in such improbable places as the Vatican archives; audiences with the Kaiser himself; reports referring both to his prowess as a naval officer and to his 'diplomatic missions', none of which had the status of what is usually thought of as a diplomatic mission and which were probably much more deadly in their purpose.

In appearance, Canaris was of medium height and had conventional good looks. His speech was hesitant, his manner somewhat ingratiating. A nonentity, one would have said. Perhaps it is too often forgotten that the best spies are by definition shadowy persons who escape notice by virtue of their uninteresting grayness. It would never have crossed a casual observer's mind that here was a man who had had adventures of some magnitude.

He continued to have them after the war. On the proclamation of the Republic by Scheidemann in November 1918 (formally constituted by the Assembly at Weimar in July 1919) Canaris declared his loyalty to the President, Chancellor, and Army High Command and immediately set about betraying them. He had a hand in the persecution and murder of the Spartacist revolutionaries Karl Liebnecht and Rosa Luxemburg and also – when the tables were turned and he found himself linked with the clandestine band of plotters being accused of murder – convincingly dissociated himself from the plot. He also managed, despite his oath of allegiance to the Republic, to join forces with that section of the army that planned to restore the Kaiser and the Hohenzollern traditions and trample the hated Socialist régime into the dust. The proposed trampling was aided in a practical way by funds and weapons that Canaris eased out of the Baltic Naval Station's accounts and stores.

Now, in 1922, with the arrival on the Kiel scene of the conveniently musical Heydrich, Canaris was engaged in yet another surreptitious activity; the rebuilding of the German armed forces. The Versailles Treaty which, after undergoing many vicissitudes at the hands and tempers of the members of the League of Nations, was signed at last in June 1919, of course expressly forbade any such rearmament; so arrangements had to be made with sympathetic countries to produce weapons and ships. Canaris engineered contracts with, and payments to, the ship-yards of several neutral countries including Spain, where submarines and torpedoes could be made and stored until the time came to use them. The Spartacists were not the only revolutionary spirits in Germany. Heydrich's was not a revolutionary spirit; but his ambition to achieve personal power was evident. Canaris, who was strong on the psychological assessment of character as all schemers must be, did not fail to recognize a potential conspirator who, enthused by Canaris's own narratives of espionage, was malleable material. He made it his business to see that the young cadet was given the right sort of good reports. He also contrived circumstances in which Heydrich became a partner in a brief affair with a homosexual naval officer. There was evidence in the form of letters and photographs, and of these Canaris secured copies. One never knew when events would necessitate a turn toward blackmail; and even though Heydrich had been a victim rather than a willing partner, circumstantial evidence could be directed in more than one way. The negatives were carefully stored in Canaris's safe and a hint dropped to Heydrich as to their existence if not of their whereabouts. In the folder was a note recording that 'Heydrich did not respond altogether as I expected. His reaction was to reveal a brooding hatred of the homosexual type rather than a fear of the consequences'. It was a reaction that was to have its consequences.

Canaris need not have bothered about any tendency on Heydrich's part to need the persuasion of blackmail to keep him under his master's thumb. He was a willing apprentice in the arts of conspiracy. Also, his reasoning was subtle enough to perceive that in that direction haste must be made slowly: a foundation of routine achievement was the first essential. To that end he applied himself unsparingly to the syllabus of navigation, gunnery, signals, wireless telegraphy and other normal nautical matters and at the end of 1924 he was made a midshipman. 'An outstandingly successful cadet', his report noted, 'with a particular aptitude for languages that suggests a posting in due course to the Intelligence staff'.

'In due course' turned out to be July 1928, by which time he was a full lieutenant. Canaris's string-pulling had resulted in Heydrich becoming, in his own words 'a member of the Admiral's staff at Kiel as a signals officer in Naval Intelligence'. The Admiral was Erich Raeder, who became, in 1939, Grand Admiral and commander-in-chief of the German navy under Hitler. For the time being, however, he was a Staff Officer in Berlin with a very close interest in the secret rebuilding of the German navy. 'I saw in Heydrich', he wrote in his memoirs, 'a young man with far to go and great abilities'.

Everyone, in fact, seems to have been impressed by Heydrich and his future naval career. But that career was to have an untimely end.

By 1930 he had passed all his examinations, been promoted chief signals officer, and acquired enough fluency in English, French and Russian to prepare him for Canaris's widening Intelligence network. But his main off-duty activity had continued to be the pursuit of women; and in the summer of that year he had a brief affair with one girl and a more lasting

Above: The German Navy expands. *Berlin* commissioned as a cruiser. *Left: Admiral Scheer. Right:* The U-Boat arm grows. *Below:* Admiral Erich Raeder

one with another. The brief encounter was with the daughter of a steel magnate, Otto Schlueter, but it was not so brief as to have no consequences, and early in 1931 she told him she was pregnant. By that time, however, he had become engaged to Lina von Osten, aged nineteen and the daughter of a schoolmaster from Fehmarn Island in the Baltic. There was a showdown between Schlueter and Heydrich in which every melodramatic stop was pulled out by the outraged father, including threats of horse-whipping and ruination of Heydrich's career unless he married the girl – no idle threat, to be sure, for Schlueter was a personal friend of both Canaris and Raeder and had supplied some of the money for secret rearmament funds. He was a powerful man as well as an apoplectic one.

According to the betrayed girl, who remained tearfully present throughout the interview, Heydrich remained icily calm, refused to marry her because 'it would not be in accordance with the honour of a naval officer if he were to break off his engagement so long as Lina von Osten remained willing to marry him', clicked his heels and bowed in salute and left the house.

This highly emotional to-do was by no means the end of the matter – as indeed it hardly could be with such an outraged parent. Schlueter went to Raeder and demanded justice for his daughter – a demand that the Admiral was in no position to refuse if he wanted to continue to receive Schlueter's secret economic help in rearming Germany, which of course he did. He gave Heydrich a direct order to marry the compromised girl, failing which he would be court-martialled and dismissed the navy. Heydrich doggedly repeated his refusal to break off his engagement to Lina von Osten unless she herself wished to end the betrothal (which she very firmly did

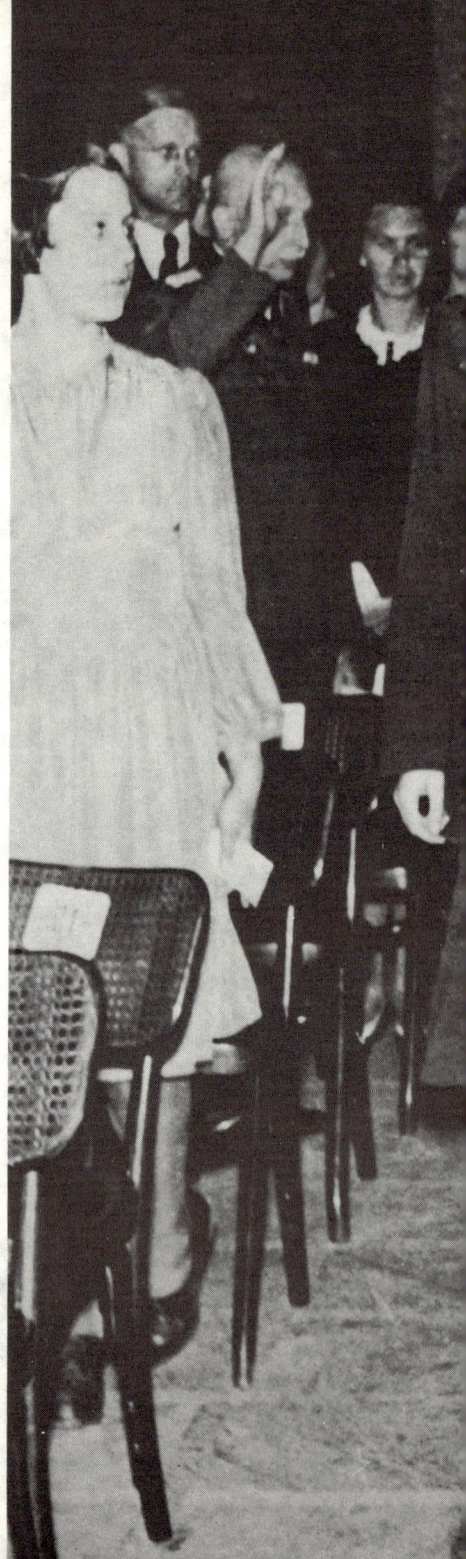

Heydrich with his wife, the last picture taken before his assassination

not), and accepted the court-martial, whose verdict could scarcely be other than it was. 'At the end of April 1931', he wrote in a précis of his career which he submitted to his later employer, Himmler, 'I was dismissed the service on non-service grounds by a court-of-honour decision that was ratified by the Reich President' – who was at that time Field Marshal von Hindenburg.

One must concede that in the melodramatic circumstances prevailing his action was as stiffly correct as that of Otto Schlueter. So also was the rigid opposition of von Osten, who was determined that his daughter should not marry 'an immoral scoundrel who threatened to take God knew what sins of impurity to the bed of his virgin daughter' – as Canaris amusedly recorded. His determination was matched, however, by an equal determination on Lina's part, and in the end it was his that was undone. She was married to Heydrich on 26th December 1931 – though with few hopes for the future, for her new husband was a cashiered naval officer with no money and no prospect of any job in a country which was one of the centres of the world economic crisis and in which six million unemployed had been drawn into the vortex of poverty. It says much for her strength of character that the marriage did not

The Mayor of Munich is arrested by Freikorps and SA units

founder in its early months, not only for economic reasons but also because Heydrich was revealing characteristics that had thus far remained obscured by his overt romanticism. Nervous irritability, extremely bitter cynicism and calculating iciness combined to make a sinister if blurred negative of her snapshot view of Heydrich as a romantic and staunchly honourable hero. She also soon had evidence that marriage had in no way diminished his sexual lusts outside that exalted state. Of that she was tolerant. Heydrich was demonstrably in love with her, and in a way that at that time was considered daring she made allowances for the male spouse's peccadilloes. She was far less tolerant about his lack of a job. Though realizing the difficulties imposed by the economic crisis she was determined that his talents should be guided along the right course. And that course, she believed, was politics. It can truly be said in the light of subsequent events that Lina von Osten has much to answer for.

Heydrich's politics, as such, could up to that time have been considered non-existent. 'He was not a political animal', his wife said in a 1957 interview. 'He was just a professional naval staff officer. His only other interests were music and sport. He knew nothing about politics at all; nor did he want to.' And it is true that his youthful association with the *Freikorps* was, as has been hinted, an experiment in the art of achieving power by way of thuggery, rather than support for the politics of the wide-ranging revolutionaries who were running amok in Germany's streets in the years following the country's defeat – if, indeed, many such organizations could themselves be said to have any politics but the politics of violence. Heydrich's affiliations, such as they were, were to the traditional Hohenzollern background of his parents, as was natural considering his upbringing and schooling.

Lina von Osten, on the other hand, was a fanatical supporter of a political party that had emerged into the murky light of post-war Germany while she was still a schoolgirl: the Nazi party of Adolf Hitler. She was not merely a supporter, she was a party member – with the number 1201380, and like the increasing thousands who in metaphor flung themselves at the feet of the Austrian lance-corporal, she knew no joy greater than that of listening to, and absorbing, the Führer's strident analyses of the nation's troubles and his panaceas for their cure, both of

Reichsführer SS Heinrich Himmler

which in 1932 were strident indeed. And within the party, she told Heydrich, was a *corps d'élite* that would not only welcome his highly disciplined training as a naval officer but would welcome it in the most satisfactory way – with a paid job.

The mention of a *corps d'élite* did not impress Heydrich; nor did Hitler's schemes for the establishment of a New and Greater German Reich. Though he had himself been involved with banditry, he thought of it as a gentlemanly banditry in which the lower orders had their heads bashed together to teach them a lesson. Hitler, he was uncomfortably aware, was aiming at a wider influence and gaining it. Bruno Heydrich, in the days when Hitler had created active trouble in an abortive *Putsch* and landed himself in jail for it, had referred to the Nazi leader as 'an upstart parvenu'. It was clearly the proper classification for such a man and Heydrich, with his acquired naval snobbery and lack of political interests, despised him.

But Lina had one more trick to play. The upper crust, she pointed out, were extremely interested in the Nazi movement because they saw in it the possibility of the restoration of the German feudal system; not only that; there was an even closer personal link: the Baron Friederich von Eberstein, who had been one of Bruno Heydrich's pupils and whose mother was Reinhard's godmother, had recently joined the *corps d'élite* and would willingly arrange, as she had established by writing to him, for Heydrich to have an interview with its chief, one Heinrich Himmler.

In this way, by force of circumstances and the subtle designs of his wife, Heydrich was manoeuvred into the Nazi party, which he joined as a necessary preliminary to arranging an interview with Himmler, on 8th June 1932.

Above: Friederich von Eberstein, who helped manoeuvre Heydrich into the Nazi Party. ***Below:*** Hitler in Landsberg prison

The Führer at Nuremberg, 1934. Heydrich has become one of the inner-court

Nazi

Early SS members in Berlin, and (right) in Nuremberg

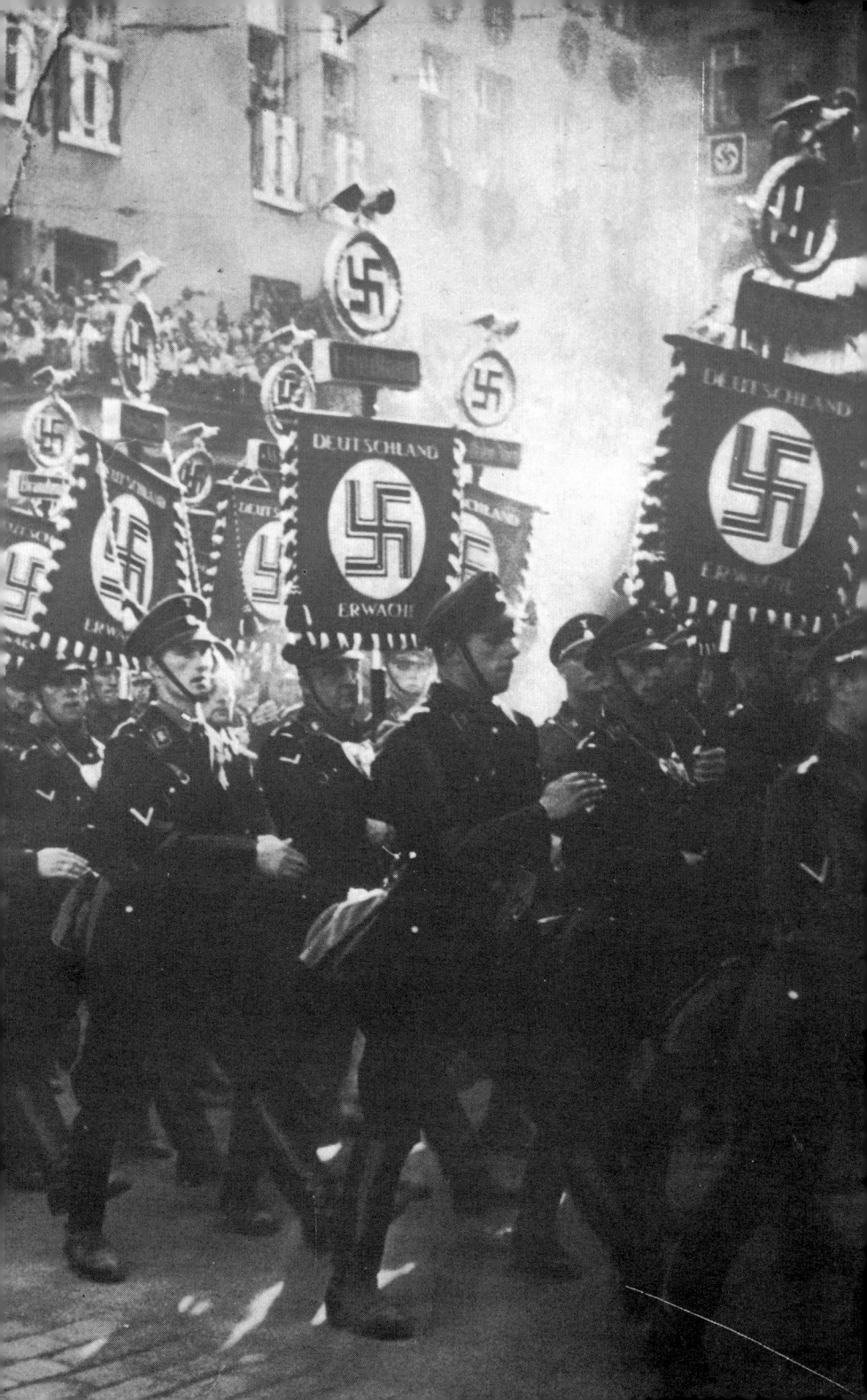

The *corps d'élite* to which Heydrich somewhat reluctantly gave his attention was the *Schutzstaffel;* more commonly, and later more terribly, known as the SS. It could not have had less elite origins. A decade earlier, when Hitler had been fighting for recognition of his *Nationalsozialistische Deutsche Arbeiterpartei* (National Socialist German Workers' Party), which cumbersome title had been snipped down to Nazi, he had needed a bodyguard to protect him in the frequent brawls that accompanied his electioneering. There was of course the private revolutionary militia of the party, the brown-shirted Storm Troops (*Sturmabteilung* or SA); but these were the front-line action men. 'I told myself', Hitler wrote in *Mein Kampf*, 'that I needed a bodyguard, even a very restricted one. But it had to be made up of men who would enlist without conditions, willing to march even against their brothers – only twenty of them to a city, and of absolute reliability rather than a doubtful mass'. So in each major city a score or so of men were enlisted as protection men and shock troops.

The SS's small numerical strength was its salvation, just as the unrestricted size and unruliness of the SA was its undoing when, in 1923, Hitler attempted to wrest power from the Bavarian government in the *Putsch* of 9th November. After his trial for treason and subsequent imprisonment the Nazi party was banned, SA and all; but the diminutive SS with only 200 members was overlooked. So when Hitler was released after serving only eight months of his five-year sentence he still had his small body of fanatical SS loyalists awaiting him. In 1926 the ban on the SA was raised and the SS, though differentiated by its uniform of black and silver, was absorbed into the larger formation.

Leadership of the SS was given by Hitler to the Bavarian nonentity Heinrich Himmler in January 1929. Himmler had become an SS member in 1925 and his new appointment as

Reichsführer-SS filled him with joy. Not only did he long for grandiose titles, he saw also an opportunity in his new appointment for indulging his mania for assembling and indexing information, for he planned to extend the scope of the *corps d'élite*.

Which indeed he did. He expanded its strength, laid down its ideological rules, organized its physical tests, and planned to divide its operations into departments with specific purposes. It was in connexion with one

SA propaganda vehicle on a recruiting drive

of these purposes that he interviewed Heydrich.

The interview was important not only as the occasion on which Heydrich was established as an officer of the SS, but also as the beginning of his personal relationship with Himmler. The two of them were birds of a feather in their concern with other people's characteristics and foibles and the advantages that could be gained from secret information, though their purposes diverged in that Himmler's concern was ideological while Heydrich's was self-interested – not in the mercenary sense in which Canaris's had been self-interested, but because the accumulation of facts about people over whom he could gain control inflated his ego.

He had preceded the interview with Himmler by having a long session

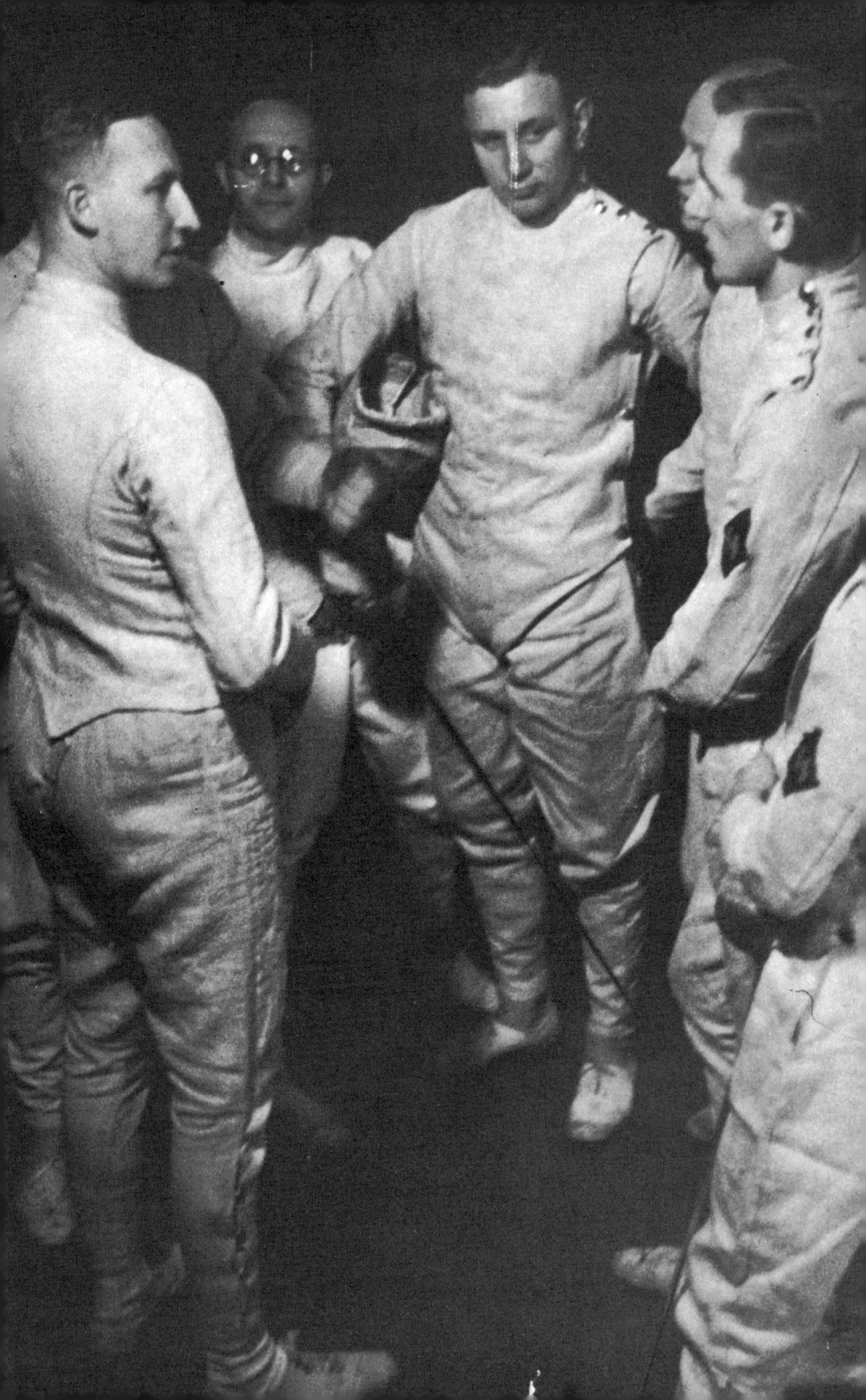

with von Eberstein. The Baron had become thoroughly indoctrinated by Nazi ideals – which, Hitler had found, could be easily adjusted to fit the needs of a variety of classes and professions. Von Eberstein's indoctrination resulted in a transmissable enthusiasm. He was able to convince Heydrich that far from being the ideological claptrap of a parvenu vulgarian, Nazism was the only way back to power of the traditionalists and upper classes of the Hohenzollern empire. In a long analysis of Hitler's achievements and plans for the future it appeared to Heydrich that there was greater power in the hierarchy of the Nazi party than even the navy had offered. It is certain that he was less interested in the restoration of German grandeur than in his personal advancement. But if Germany too could profit by his achievements they would be doubly laudable. No doubt he graciously conceded that; he was an arrogant man.

The interview with Himmler went well. The *Reichsführer-SS* was in many ways a stupid man; but he recognized in the icy personality of the elegantly dressed Heydrich a kindred spirit. 'He is a man of scruples and of no scruples', he recorded cryptically in his diary. 'One cannot imagine him ever coming to terms with half-measures. Also, there is the matter of his ancestry, which could prove a very definite advantage'.

Himmler was referring to the fact, which he had of course been wily enough to establish by way of his many paid informants, that Heydrich was tainted with Jewish blood. His maternal grandmother, Sarah Mautsch, had migrated from Nuremberg, where her family lived in the Jewish quarter, to Dresden and married Eugen Krantz there in 1863. She had brought a considerable dowry and that had alleviated any anti-Semitic feeling the Krantzes might have had – though there is no reason for supposing that they were in any way bothered about the influx of Jewish blood. 'Rich Grandmother Mautsch' was referred to without hostility by the Krantzes and later by the Heydrichs. And to Reinhard Heydrich, according to his wife Lina, the matter of his Jewish grandmother 'was neither here nor there'. In conforming to the antisemitism of the party that offered so much scope for personal power he was to display a remarkable change of heart.

Himmler in his ferrety way had discovered the taint in the ancestry of his interviewee. But with typical cunning he said nothing of it. He did not want the possibilities for blackmail to escape him by blurting them out before Heydrich was in his clutches. He told Heydrich that he had had reports of his excellence as a naval Intelligence Officer (which in fact Heydrich had never been) and had something similar in mind for him in the SS.

What he had in mind was the establishment of an Intelligence bureau that would not only collate more efficiently the innumerable items of information that were collected by innumerable spies and agents of varying degrees of responsibility, but would also have the backing of the highest authority in taking action against those who for one reason or another fell foul of the régime. He was in fact taking the first step toward forming the force of secret police without which no dictatorship can function; though Hitler was not yet even in power.

Heydrich had to pass what Himmler thought of as an aptitude test; but since it consisted only of a brief indication, written in twenty minutes, of the way Heydrich thought a Nazi Intelligence service should be formed and run, it put little strain on his abilities. 'True Intelligence', he wrote succinctly, 'is in its ideal form the acquisition of every scrap of information about the enemy and the pre-

The great tradition: Heydrich in fencing class

vention of the reverse of that situation. Security is every bit as urgent as espionage'.

It was in fact as a security service that Heydrich's splinter group of Himmler's SS was established. It was called the *Sicherheitsdienst*, literally Security Police Duty, quickly abbreviated to SD, and it began functioning in Munich, where its office was at Turkenstrasse 23. Heydrich's salary as a *Scharführer* or junior lieutenant of the SS was RM 180 (about $40) a month – a sum that can hardly have allowed him and Lina to live in style. But Lina could not with justification blame him for that; nor did she. Her fanaticism and pride in her husband's establishment in the *corps d'élite* of the party were enough.

In this year before Hitler's achievement of dictatorial power the SS was still a division of the embarrassingly large and disorderly SA. Under Himmler's leadership it had increased its membership to nearly 50,000 men who were 'the best physically, the most faithful, and the most dependable members of the Nazi movement'. It was Himmler's design that it should be used, first, to subdue the influence of the SA; secondly through Heydrich's *Sicherheitsdienst* to spy on all party members and officials from the highest to the lowest (even including Hitler himself); thirdly, to inculcate the crackpot racial theories of Houston Stewart Chamberlain, Walter Darré, Alfred Rosenberg and similar lunatics; and finally to enable him to gain control of the civil police system (a position he coveted) and the *Abwehr*, the Intelligence System of the armed forces that Canaris had been at such great pains to rebuild under the very eye of the League of Nations.

So far as evidence to undermine the influence of the SA was concerned there was speedy good news.

'Such evidence', Heydrich reported

Above: Heydrich joins the SS leadership.
Right: Hitler with the rival leaders; Röhm to his right, and Himmler

to Himmler, 'will not be difficult to come by. The SA leadership is riddled with monstrous, bloated, homosexual cretins.'

A mild exaggeration perhaps; but its leader, Ernst Röhm, was certainly bloated and unequivocally homosexual. And its staff and soldiery were in the main coarse thugs – many of them having been recruited from the *Freikorps*. This was the point in Heydrich's career at which he turned violently against his own origins and affiliations. Possibly he despised himself for ever having belonged to such a ragtag-and-bobtail organization as the *Freikorps*, which had blossomed (though that was scarcely the word) into this uncontrollable, and therefore dangerous, private army. 'It is too willing to act for the Strasser brothers', Heydrich continued, 'and the Führer's bitterest enemies are those two traitors.' Otto and Gregor Strasser, it was true, were sometime adherents of the Nazi party and Otto had hived off to set up an anti-Nazi organization in Prague. Gregor had kept the party alive below ground during the period of Hitler's jail sentence and had been a rival for the leadership, and in Himmler's mind still was; which gave the sycophantic *Reichsführer-SS* a chance to demonstrate his devotion to Hitler. He did so by presenting in person a wordy report which was a consolidation of Heydrich's observations and his own plans for the future growth of the SS – which, he assured Hitler, 'could be built into an organization ready at any time to take over the entire machinery of government, and even at this moment [1932] could deal adequately with all individuals and organizations hostile to the Nazi movement.' As a makeweight of information thrown in to draw attention to his own perspicacity, he told Hitler that he now had in his employ as a staff officer one Reinhard Heydrich

Gregor Strasser

who had 'a partially Jewish ancestry which will prove useful in holding him to faith with the party, since he will always be grateful that we have overlooked the matter of his impurity or alternatively we can at any time force him into submission by threats of disclosure'.

Hitler's *Table Talk* records that he was fully in agreement with the wisdom of Himmler's machinations; but he made a proviso: Heydrich must be told that knowledge of his impure racial strain was in the records – otherwise he might deny or suppress it.

In a soothing talk in which Himmler adopted what he meant to be a fatherly manner (he was only four years older than Heydrich) he let fall the observation that 'any contamination of the blood two generations back was scarcely important and would in any case be eliminated in Heydrich's own children'. (Lina was pregnant with her first child.)

'His reaction', Himmler wrote in his journal, 'was surprising. "I intend to eliminate the strain myself", he said. "No-one has a greater contempt for Jews than I have". His eyes glinted and his long thin hands made a gesture of scornfully sweeping away everything in their path.'

What his long thin hands actually swept away at this stage was the documentary evidence of his Jewish taint. His plans for the elimination of Judaism from the Nazi world would follow later. As the controller of the *Sicherheitsdienst* he had no difficulty in getting access to registers of births, marriages and deaths and he effectively obliterated all references to Sarah Mautsch, so that any investigation into his genealogy would be frustrated by lack of evidence. In a régime riddled with spies the destruction of evidence gives the suspect every advantage, just as in the country of the blind the one-eyed man is king.

Power

The accessories of secrecy were indispensable to Heydrich. Codes, safes, skeleton keys, indexes, miniature cameras, peepholes, hidden microphones and recording apparatus, disguises, aliases – they excited him, according to Walter Schellenberg (with whom he was to become closely associated), 'almost sexually'. His spoken sentences, pitched in his rather feminine voice, invariably tailed off before they were completed, as if he were reluctant to reveal the extent of his thoughts, as if anything put into actual words compromised the wariness that should modify all communication. After all, he had written, 'Security is every bit as urgent as espionage'.

That being so, it was in no way puzzling that he should accomplish the retrieval of the evidence relating to the contrived homosexual affair between himself and the Signals Lieutenant who had been his dominating partner – evidence that was secreted in Canaris's safe – with admirable ingenuity. Like the evidence of his tainted blood it had to be swept away from the path to power.

For some months he planned the little operation, taking as much trouble as he did years later when he contrived the incident of the radio station that provided the excuse for Hitler's armies to attack Poland.

Himmler's files held information that was classified and cross-indexed so thoroughly that it was possible to find anything in a few seconds. The hundreds of thousands of index cards were stored in metal compartments mounted on a huge circular revolving table which, by pressing a button, could bring any section before the operator. Using this apparatus it took Heydrich very little time to locate the dossier of a cracksman whose safe-breaking past, as demonstrated by his avoidance of arrest, had been highly successful. Nor was it difficult, once the man was found, to arrange that he make two burglarious entries into Canaris's house – the first to photograph the Heydrich package so that an externally similar one could be prepared to replace it, the second to steal the package; and both of which were undetected. It was a little more difficult to ensure the safe-breaker's subsequent silence; but when he was found dead in an alleyway a few days later there was nothing to connect the death with Heydrich, who indeed had had nothing to do with it except to order it.

Thus with proper care two potential stumbling blocks had been removed from the way. There might be – in fact were – many gossipy rumours reflecting on his career in the future; even one or two actual legal actions; but by that time he was in an invincible position and enemies who risked action did so at their peril and got flung into concentration camps for defamation or had to shell out heavy fines.

Meanwhile Adolf Hitler was battering his way to power. He was appointed the twenty-second Chancellor of the German Republic on 30th January 1933; and when Paul von Hindenburg died, senile in mind and body, on 2nd August 1934, Hitler made haste to seize the Presidency and the

Otto Strasser, still the youthful soldier

leadership of the armed forces and thus to decome Dictator of Germany. His progress to absolute despotism was considerably eased by the machinations of Himmler's SS in which, still, was concealed the *Sicherheitsdienst*. Of Heydrich's dangerously influential organization everything that was then unsuspected outside the Himmler-Heydrich entourage was to be confirmed years later by Gideon Hausner, Israel's Attorney-General, when he opened for the prosecution at the trial of Karl Adolf Eichmann, head of Heydrich's so-called 'Office for Jewish Emigration', which was concerned with extermination rather than emigration.

'The satanic force which was Nazism', Hausner said, 'constructed its own instruments of rule with great thoroughness and fiendish cunning... The SD... was described as "the brains of the Party and the State". It was an internal espionage and detective organization which did not balk at any means for achieving its purposes. Heydrich, who organized and commanded this service, always contended: "One must know as much as possible about people". For that purpose he set up his Party Intelligence System to include confidential agents (*V-Leute*), ordinary agents (*A-Leute*), informers (*Z-Leute*), casual employees (*H-Leute*), and doubtful informants (*U-Leute*). They were happy to receive any information whatsoever about economic developments, social life, politics, and, especially, about the private lives of Party members. Heydrich wanted to know every possible detail about the members of the Party and their opponents, everything relating to their character and weaknesses; their hobbies and habits; scandals in which they had been involved; their personal desires and love life; the places they frequented; the expenditures and incomes of industrial firms, the movements of bank deposits

Hitler, then Chancellor, with President Hindenburg in 1933

After Hindenburg's death, Hitler becomes dictator

– in brief, every item that might be exploited, in one way or another, against a man or an institution, especially if it might be used as a threat for purposes of blackmail. All this was patiently and thoroughly collected and recorded. Nothing in the most intimate lives of all the leaders of the Reich, and afterwards of the leaders and administrators of the whole of Europe, escaped the vigilance of the SD. Clearly such an instrument soon became a weapon of great strength.' A more alarming tangible weapon was being built at the same time. This was nothing less than the completely rearmed and reconstituted *Wehrmacht*. The submarines and other vessels that Canaris had ordered to be constructed in Spanish shipyards in the 1920s had long been completed and paid for by contributions from industrialists who were hoping for a return of Prussian might under a reconstructed Hohenzollern régime but were cautiously willing to accept Nazi policy as its intentions began to unfold. Others had been prefabricated in Finland and Holland and their parts stored at Kiel ready for assembly. Also, the keels of two new battle cruisers, later to become famous as the *Scharnhorst* and *Gneisenau*, had been laid down. Watchful Allied Control Commission agents were fed the information that the new vessels were to be merchantmen. Göring's rapidly expanding air force was disguised as Germany's competitive civil airline, and the training of *Luftwaffe* personnel was carried out under the aegis of the so-called League for Air Sports. As for the *stehendes Heer*, the standing army of 100,000 permitted by Versailles, it had secretly become 300,000 by the end of 1934, its vast growth theoretically concealed by the simple expedient of faking army lists.

Behind the *Wehrmacht* was a correspondingly huge growth of martial industry. Gustav Krupp of the famous

Hitler moves in diplomatic circles, with French Ambassador Poncet

armaments firm wrote, 'After the assumption of power by Adolf Hitler I had the honour to report to the Führer that Krupp stood ready after a short warm-up to begin the rearmament of the German people'. As indeed the firm did. 'The 'short warm-up' in fact occupied much of the 1920s, during which, according to William Manchester in *The Arms of Krupp*, 'American Intelligence officers had found that of recent [Krupp] patents 26 were for artillery control devices, 18 for electrical fire control apparatus, 9 for fuses and shells, 17 for field guns, and 14 for heavy cannon which could be moved only by rail'. Their information was ignored, partly through dilatoriness, partly because the Treaty did not prohibit drawing-board design as distinct from manufacture. Also, it was quite simple to classify blueprints for tanks, self-propelled guns and mobile mortars as various kinds of 'agricultural tractors'. And even easier to turn out, from plants ultimately intended for small-arms manufacture, such innocent products as bicycles, perambulators, lawn mowers, cash registers and the like. There was such a profusion of these in the Essen works of Krupp that Control Commission officers remarked encouragingly in Germany's industrious determination to achieve economic recovery. Since all the dates of their 'unannounced' inspections were ferreted out by Heydrich's agents and telegraphed in code, it was not difficult to prepare the deceptive façade of peaceful industry.

It was not possible, however, for Hitler's preparations for war to be indefinitely concealed. Even the dullest of diplomats and observers could not be fooled for ever; and it was clear to the Allies by late 1934 that there was a great deal going on in Germany that did not fall under the heading of 'economic reconstruction'. There was a prompt, and not even particularly grudging, recognition by the British government, in the person of its

Foreign Secretary, Sir John Simon, that Germany was entitled to parity of arms with other European countries. This peculiar disregard of the Versailles Treaty was implemented in February 1935 by a proposal to grant Germany complete arms equality in return for Hitler's agreement to 'a general European settlement'. Whatever that may have meant to Hitler it certainly did not mean any bargaining for the right to rearm Germany – which rearmament was in any case virtually a *fait accompli*. Göring frankly and delightedly told the London *Daily Mail*'s correspondent Ward Price that Germany's rapidly developing 'civil airline' was in fact a fully armed and fully trained air force ready for battle.

'With whom?' Ward Price asked in astonishment. He had recently written a series of articles intended to convince his readers, whom he must have taken to be mentally deficient and morally decadent (both of which to some extent they were), that Germany's problems could not be settled by war, that Hitler had personally told him that war would not come again, and that the nation was 'in a state of profound peace'.

Chuckling, Göring replied that the question could be answered only 'by those who wish to wage war on Nazi Germany'. Reassured, the blissfully blinkered Ward Price told his readers that there was no sane country that wished to do that 'and set the world aflame with the holocaust of war again', and that therefore everyone could relax once more.

Which a good many of them did. Whereupon Hitler announced on 16th March 1935 that he had re-introduced conscription and planned a peacetime army of 500,000 men. That drew from the League of Nations a great deal of tut-tutting and the formation of a committee charged with preventing any such warlike measures in future. Upon which flaccid action Hitler with-

Scharnhorst and **Gneisenhau** are launched

The Luftwaffe expands

The armaments begin to flow

drew Germany from the League and in place of her membership offered a declaration of peace:

'Whoever lights the torch of war in Europe can wish for nothing but chaos. We, however, live in the firm conviction that in our time will be fulfilled not the decline but the renaissance of the West. That Germany may make an imperishable contribution to this great work is our proud hope and our unshakable belief'.

Geoffrey Dawson, the editor of the London *Times*, said in a leader that could be compared only with the soothing syrup of an indulgent Nanny, that:

'The speech turns out to be reasonable, straightforward and comprehensive. No-one who reads it with an impartial mind can doubt that the points of policy laid down by Herr Hitler may fairly constitute . . . a sincere and well-considered utterance . . .'

Herr Hitler's well-considered utterance quickly turned itself into a new naval 'agreement' in which Britain betrayed both France and Italy by accepting that Germany should begin immediately to expand her navy to one third the strength of Britain's, which meant in practice that Hitler could gleefully carry on with building five battleships, twenty-one cruisers and sixty-four destroyers, plus an unlimited number of submarines, and in terms of tonnage could bring the German navy into a supreme position. These vessels were the ones that when war came were to cause Britain such disastrous losses in the battle of the Atlantic.

The Anglo-German naval agreement also gave Mussolini licence to treat the League of Nations covenant with as much contempt as Britain, her perfidious ally, had shown in formulating it. His invasion of Abyssinia in October 1935 brought more tut-tutting

Krupp

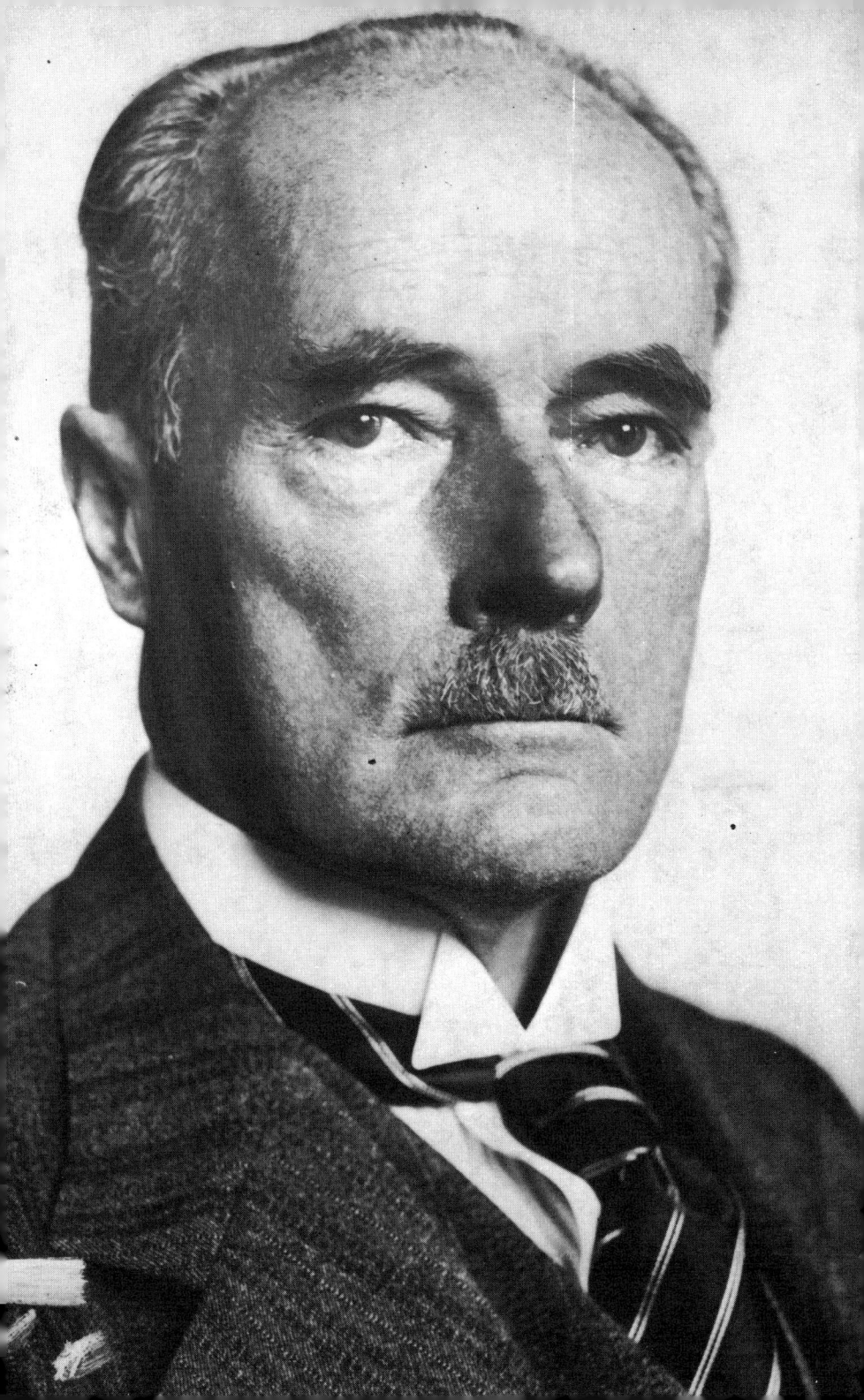

Above: Sir John Simon. *Right:* Göring with Himmler, 1932

Italy invades Abyssinia

from London and a sort of whining noise from Paris. These flourished wanly into an imposition of sanctions on Italy, which in turn snipped asunder the tenuous, not to mention suspicious, cordiality of Mussolini's Fascists towards France and Britain.

The Foreign Correspondent in Berlin of the *Chicago Tribune*, William Shirer, noted in his diary the day after Mussolini's *coup*:

'The Wilhelmstrasse is delighted. Either Mussolini will stumble and get himself so heavily involved in Africa that he will be greatly weakened in Europe, whereupon Hitler can seize Austria, hitherto protected by the Duce; or he will win, defying France and Britain and thereupon be ripe for a tie-up with Hitler against the Western Democracies. Either way Hitler wins'.

Perspicacious words, as it proved.

Concurrently with Hitler's dictatorial climb to power and his seizure of every opportunity that opened to him to achieve his megalomaniac ends, Heydrich was engineering, rather more insidiously, his own achievement of personal power within the Nazi ranks. His was a name that was unknown to the statesmen of Europe and was rarely heard even in Germany. Hitler, Göring, Goebbels, Bormann and Hess were the Big Five, their names ever in the headlines, their speeches booming from the inescapable public address systems and flaring in the columns of the totalitarian press. But it was not the power of publicity that Heydrich wanted. The reverse, the subtler power of secrecy, was his objective.

His first big step toward it was made at Hitler's first Cabinet meeting after his appointment as Chancellor. It was an appointment at the time almost unnoticed by those whom it was to affect the most, and the background to it needs a word of clarification.

Mussolini

Heydrich with Nazi Party Leaders, 1936

A characteristic of the German Reich under the Hohenzollerns was its division into states and principalities, each with, among other autonomies, its own police force. The largest of the states was Prussia, which had in addition a secret political police force, Bureau IA, that fell into Göring's hands when, at Hitler's first Cabinet meeting, he was appointed Prime Minister and Minister of the Interior of Prussia. Bureau IA was renamed *Geheime Staatspolizei* (Secret State Police) trimmed to Gestapo for convenience' sake, and Göring used it for rounding up and disposing of – by murder or 'protective custody' in concentration camps – political opponents of Nazism.

There was a similar secret police force in Bavaria, and it was to the command of this that Heydrich was appointed. It had far too little influence for his taste and as a first step he amalgamated it with the SD and then, with the backing of Himmler and the SS, he gradually swallowed up the political departments – they were not dignified by any more impressive designation – of the civil forces of numerous smaller autonomies throughout Germany. It was the second step in the growth of the police state. Himmler had taken the first step with his establishment of the SD; his protégé was forcing its sinister sap through the arteries of totalitarianism.

Munich, the capital of Bavaria and the birthplace of the Nazi party, provided Heydrich with the man who was to become his deputy and chief of the Gestapo when the influence of that insidious enterprise had permeated throughout the Reich. His name was Heinrich Müller, and he was an ordinary police officer – an inspector – who had been transferred to the political branch in the early days of the Nazis, when the SA thugs had been involved

Hitler's first picture as Chancellor

Hitler with Propaganda Minister Goebbels

in brawls in every street and beer hall. In those days he had been, not unnaturally, a fanatical opponent of Nazism; and in trying to curtail the SA's activities had made a special study of the Russian OGPU. It was this esoteric knowledge that Heydrich saw as an invaluable addition to his own. He had no difficulty in persuading Müller to turn his coat. In the intervening years had had considerably modified his political views, though he had never become a party member; and indeed never did. But there was in any case a matter of some consequence that had been tucked well away into Müller's background and which Himmler's meticulously complied dossiers had revealed: like Heydrich he was tainted with Jewish blood; but unlike the new Munich police chief and head of the SD, he had been unable to dispose of the evidence.

'I confronted him', Heydrich told Himmler, who recorded it in his journal, 'with the alarming confirmation that the Jews were not going to

At Carinhall, Göring's country home, for the burial of his first wife Carin

Heinrich Müller

Above: Martin Bormann
Right and over page: The concentration camps begin to fill

have a very comfortable time and that it might be as well for knowledge of his ancestry to be kept dark. He was very accommodating, therefore, in the matter of offering his services to the Gestapo'. 'He should prove as trustworthy as Heydrich himself', Himmler added.

In no sense except as an enemy of those who stood in his way was Heydrich ever trustworthy. Nor did he trust anybody. His personal life was a reproduction in miniature of the incessant struggle for power that typifies every totalitarian state and its inner rivalries, forever grinding each other down as they battle for supremacy. His schizophrenic hatred of his Jewish ancestry manifested itself in full-scale activity of the most monstrous kind against Judaism in general. Unlike his nominal master, Himmler, he had no cranky ideological ideas about purity of race. His vindictiveness was personal and unlimited.

Schellenberg says:

'His cold eyes glinted with icy pleasure when he gave directions for a Jewish family of shopkeepers, who had been discovered by the Gestapo in some minor commercial misdemeanour, to be transported to Dachau and murdered by whipping and strangulation.'

It was evidently a form of self-flagellation by proxy. Müller reported to Himmler that at a drunken party Heydrich had accidentally cut himself on a broken glass and gleefully watched the arterial blood spurting out as he murmured 'something about "exit the filthy little corpuscles of the grandmother" while the blood splashed the walls and everyone dashed about looking for a tourniquet'.

Such occasions were rare. Heydrich was a heavy drinker, but alcohol seldom had on him the effect of loosening his tongue. Rather, it released what inhibitions he had against plotting. 'After a drunken orgy', says Rudolf Diels in *Lucifer ante Portas*, 'one always knew that there would be new schemes for liquidating enemies or supposed enemies'. And Alan Bullock in his introduction to Schellenberg's memoirs re-states a truth that is unforgettable:

'The power of a totalitarian régime rests on twin foundations: propaganda and terror. The instrument of terror in Hitler's Germany was the *Reichssicherheitshauptamt*. the Main Security Office, set up in September 1939 to bring into a single organization the Gestapo and the SS *Sicherheitsdienst*. The Main Security Office was the creation of Reinhard Heydrich, Himmler's sinister lieutenant. . . . It concentrated under the control of half a dozen men all the powers of spying and intelligence, interrogation and execution on which dictatorship ultimately rests.'

Power indeed.

Jewish business premises come under attack

Feud

The infamous 'Night of the Long Knives' was in fact the weekend of 28th June–1st July 1934. During those four days Hitler ordered the murder of all his known enemies and reduced the threatening power of the SA to virtually nothing. The brown-shirted militia that had fought his street battles from the days of the founding of the party in Munich, and now numbered two million, had become too strong and too recalcitrant. Under the leadership of Ernst Röhm it opposed the orthodox army (the *Reichswehr*) and in doing so threatened Hitler's designs to roll Chancellorship and Presidency into one – in other words, to create an absolute Dictatorship – which he could not complete while Hindenburg was still alive and wielding, in spirit if not in flesh, a powerful influence over the army. In the event he found it easy enough, after Hindenburg's death in August, to achieve his object by way of a plebiscite, which gave him a ninety percent favourable vote; but there were many old scores to settle with potentially dangerous men like Röhm and Gregor Strasser, and the purge had become necessary quite apart from dictatorial considerations.

The necessity gave Heydrich his first big chance to display his power to the full. He and Himmler were summoned by Hitler to the Chancellery on 20th June and told that every Nazi official in all party organizations had been ordered to provide information needed by the SD to combat 'the enemies of the Reich'. To legalize the order the Führer had backed it with a decree establishing the SD as the sole political intelligence department of the party. It exercised authority over the political police of all the provinces, using the Gestapo as its operating arm, was empowered to enter homes and business premises unannounced and without warrant and to deal as its operatives thought fit with anyone upon whom fell suspicion of acting other than in the interests of the Reich.

That situation had been prepared for several months earlier by introducing into the remaining shreds of democratic law the phrase *Schutzhaft*, 'protective custody', which in effect nullified all clauses in the constitution providing for civil liberties; and it was later (in 1936) to result in a ruling by the Supreme Court that all activities of the Gestapo were above the law and could not be appealed against, since it was 'carrying out the will of the Führer and therefore could not be acting illegally'. In 1936 that final piece of the totalitarian jigsaw clicked into place with the mechanical efficiency of a Nazi salute.

Thus at the Chancellery meeting of 20th June 1934 the Himmler-Heydrich combination was given literally the power of life and death over all who could be labelled, justly or by any stretch of the imagination, 'enemies of the State'.

For Heydrich, who easily persuaded Himmler to leave the practical details of the purge to him, there was the immense satisfaction of seeing his SD and Gestapo formations operate for the first time on a national level. The roundup of anti-Nazis was easily enough organized with the aid of the

**News Extra reports
the arrest of Rohm**

Extra-Blatt

Einzelnummer 10 Pfg.

Oberbayer. Gebirgsbote, Holzkirchen • Miesbacher Anz., Miesbach • Tegernseer Ztg., Tegernsee, Aiblinger Ztg., Bad Aibling • Rosenheimer Tagbl., Rosenheim • Kolbermoorer Volksblatt, Kolbermoor • Chiemgau-Ztg., Prien • Tölzer Ztg., Bad Tölz • Wolfratshauser Tagbl., Wolfratshausen, Wasserburger Anzeiger, Wasserburg a. J. • Grafinger Zeitung, Grafing.

Samstag, 30. Juni 34

Röhm verhaftet und abgesetzt

Röhm aus Partei und S.A. ausgeschlossen

München, 30. Juni

Die Reichspressestelle der N.S.D.A.P. teilt folgende Verfügung des Führers mit:

Ich habe mit dem heutigen Tage den Stabschef Röhm seiner Stellung enthoben und aus Partei und S.A. ausgestoßen. Ich ernenne zum Chef des Stabes Obergruppenführer Lutze.

S.A.-Führer und S.A.-Männer, die seinen Befehlen nicht nachkommen oder zuwiderhandeln, werden aus S.A. und Partei entfernt bzw. verhaftet und abgeurteilt.

gez. Adolf Hitler
Oberster Partei- und S.A.-Führer

Der Führer an den neuen Stabschef

München, 30. Juni

Der Führer hat folgendes Schreiben an den Obergruppenführer der S.A. Lutze gerichtet:

An Obergruppenführer Lutze.

Mein lieber S.A.-Führer Lutze!

Schwerste Verfehlungen meines bisherigen Stabschefs zwangen mich, ihn seiner Stellung zu entheben. Sie, mein lieber Obergruppenführer Lutze, sind in vielen Jahren in guten und schlechten Tagen ein immer gleich treuer und vorbildlicher S.A.-Führer gewesen. Wenn ich Sie mit dem heutigen Tage zum Chef des Stabes ernenne, dann geschieht dies in der festen Ueberzeugung, daß es Ihrer treuen und gehorsamen Arbeit gelingen wird, aus meiner S.A. das Instrument zu schaffen, das die Nation braucht und ich mir vorstelle.

Es ist mein Wunsch, daß die S.A. zu einem treuen und starken Glied der Nationalsozialistischen Bewegung ausgebildet wird. Erfüllt von Gehorsam und blinder Disziplin, muß sie mithelfen, den neuen deutschen Menschen zu bilden und zu formen.

gez. Adolf Hitler

Aufruf des neuen Stabschefs

Der Führer hat mich an seine Seite als Chef des Stabes berufen. Das mir dadurch bewiesene Vertrauen muß und werde ich rechtfertigen durch unverbrüchliche Treue zum Führer und restlosen Einsatz für den Nationalsozialismus und dadurch für unser Volk.

Als ich vor etwa 12 Jahren zum erstenmal Führer einer kleinen S.A. war, habe ich drei Tugenden an die Spitze meines Handelns gestellt und die von der S.A. gefordert. Diese drei Tugenden haben die S.A. groß gemacht und heute, wo ich in verantwortungsvoller Stunde meinen Führer an hervorragender Stelle dienen darf, sollen sie erst recht Richtschnur für die ganze S.A. sein:

Unbedingte Treue!
Schärfste Disziplin!
Hingebender Opfermut!

So wollen wir, die wir Nationalsozialisten sind, gemeinsam marschieren.

Ich bin übergeugt, dann werden wir nur ein im Marsch zur Freiheit werden.

Es lebe der Führer! Es lebe unser Volk!

Der Chef des Stabes:
gez. Lutze

Befehl des Obersten S.A.-Führers Adolf Hitler

Adolf Hitler hat an den Chef des Stabes, Lutze, folgenden Befehl gegeben:

Wenn Sie Sie heute zum Chef des Stabes der S.A. ernenne, dann erwarte ich, daß Sie sich hier eine Reihe von Aufgaben angelegen sein lassen, die ich Ihnen hiermit stelle:

1. Ich verlange vom S.A.-Führer genau so wie vom S.A.-Mann blinden Gehorsam und unbedingte Disziplin.

2. Ich verlange, daß jeder S.A.-Führer wie jeder politische Führer sich dessen bewußt ist, daß sein Benehmen und seine Auffassung vorbildlich zu sein haben für den S.A.-Mann und für unsere gesamte Gesellschaft.

3. Ich verlange, daß der S.A.-Führer — genau so wie der politische Leiter —, die Sie in ihrem Benehmen in der Oeffentlichkeit etwas zuschulden kommen lassen, unnachsichtlich aus der Partei und der S.A. entfernt werden.

4. Ich verlange insbesondere von S.A.-Führern, daß sie ein Vorbild an Einfachheit und nicht in Aufwand ist. Ich wünsche nicht, daß der S.A.-Führer kostbare

Diners oder ähnliches teilnimmt. Man hat uns früher hierzu nicht eingeladen, wir haben auch jetzt nicht zu fordern. Millionen unserer Volksgenossen fehlt es auch heute noch am Notwendigsten zum Leben, sie sind nicht neidig auf den, den zwischen Rat und Glück sowohl angeboren groß ist, noch besonders zu vergönnen. Ich verbiete insbesondere, daß Mittel der Partei, der S.A. oder überhaupt der Oeffentlichkeit für Festlagen und dergleichen Vermendung finden. Es ist unverantwortlich, von Geldern, die zum Teil so von den Großen unserer armen Mitbürger erspart, Schwimmbäder abzustellen.

Das luxuriöse Stabs-Quartier in Berlin, in dem ein teures Einzelbett allein monatlich bis zu 30 000 Mark für Festlegen usw. ausgegeben wurden, ist sofort aufzulösen.

Ich verlange daher für alle Bartleistungen die Beranlaffung sogenannter Festlessen oder Diners aus den Tafelmitteln der S.A. Sofort verbiete ich allen Partei- und S.A.-Führern an die Teilnahme an solchen Ausgenommen davon ist nur die Erfüllung der vom Staate uns

Folgende sieben Verräter wurden bereits erschossen:

Im Zusammenhang mit dem aufgedeckten Komplott werden folgende Meuterer erschossen:

Obergruppenführer A. Schneidhuber;
Obergruppenführer Edmund Heines;
Gruppenführer Ernst, Berlin;
Gruppenführer Schmidt, München;
Gruppenführer Hans Hayn;
Gruppenführer Heydebred;
Standartenführer Graf Spretti, München.

Druck: Münchner Buchgewerbehaus M. Müller & Sohn, München.
Verantwortlich: Hauptschriftleiter W. Kettich.

'round table' and its thousands of index cards; and Heydrich told Himmler that he was 'taking the opportunity of settling a few personal scores'. That meant that the purge would include many faithful Nazis who had been doing some ferreting on their own account and had discovered clues suggesting Heydrich's tainted blood. They were to pay the price of their covert enthusiasm just as the enemies of the régime were to pay.

There had of course to be 'justification'. Himmler recorded that 'Heydrich found plenty of evidence of a threatened revolt in the ranks of the SA; it is the part of his job that he does best – this discovery of evidence of every conceivable kind, whatever the need'. And no doubt of every inconceivable kind too. In the manufacturing of lies Heydrich was in every was Dr Goebbels's equal, though their objects were different.

The actual order to 'liquidate the known enemies of the State' came from Hitler on 27th June. It was given personally to Himmler and soon after its arrival Heydrich produced the complete lists of those who were to be executed. Page after page of names was handed to the Gestapo leaders who were to visit the victims in their homes or wherever they happened to be staying and shoot them on the spot; and the commander of the SS *Leibstandarte Adolf Hitler* (whose men had sworn a special oath of personal loyalty to the Führer) in Lichterfelde barracks, Berlin, was given the names of all those who could be rounded up in the capital and stood against the barracks wall with a firing squad in the middle of the parade ground waiting only for the order to mow them down. The total number shot and otherwise disposed of during the weekend is not known; several hundreds certainly, probably nearly a thousand. Gregor Strasser, whom Hitler had never forgiven for rivalling

Hindenburg on his deathbed

him as party leader, was shot in his office; and Ernst Röhm, who epitomized for Heydrich the detested homosexuality, was dragged from his bed with his boy lover and shot as he awoke, through the head, chest and belly. Heydrich later went to view the corpse, taking with him some drunken cronies who vomited on the obese body of Hitler's sometime comrade. It was said that 'his hyena laugh as he observed the desecration of the corpse was terrifying'.

The clearest result of the purge was that the SA no longer threatened Hitler's rise to absolute power. The Defence Minister (General Werner von Blomberg), the *Reichswehr* Chief of Staff (General Werner von Fritsch), and Admiral Erich Raeder – plus, of course, Göring and his 'competitive civil airline', alias the Luftwaffe – were now ready to support Hitler in the combined rôles of President and Chancellor as soon as Hindenburg died. The brownshirts who threatened the protocol and established power of the old guard were reduced by the purge to little more than a corps of old sweats, nominally led by an ineffectual playboy called Viktor Lutze, who had betrayed Röhm to Heydrich in a message dated 28th June: 'Your man has taken a new lover, a little café pianist called Fritz-mitz. They have booked for the weekend at the Hotel Asta'. His fee for the betrayal was promotion to Chief of Staff of the now impotent Storm Troopers.

Impotent indeed, for instead of being an immense ragged organization of which the SS was merely a branch, Hitler had by decree, and as a kind of reward, freed the SS entirely from its control with only Himmler and Heydrich personally responsible to him for SS and Gestapo operations. And for his efficiency in rounding up and annihilating the SA leaders and other 'enemies of the State' (not to mention his personal enemies) Heydrich was promoted to the rank of Lieutenant-General of the SS (*Gruppenführer*). His only superior in SS rank was Him-

Above: Blomberg. *Right:* Fritsch

Angelika Raubal, Hitler's niece

mler himself; and it is true to say that except for Hitler he was the most dangerous man in Germany.

On the face of things that dubious accolade should have been Himmler's, for his was nominally the master mind. But Himmler had achieved his leadership largely because of providential circumstances. His was the lunatic evil of the ideologist to whom racial purity was the key to the new Germany. With his austere wife, his long nose for information, his herbal tea to combat his stomach cramps, his parsimonious way of living, and his weakness for titles and vain forms of grandiloquence, Himmler was a nonentity into whose hands the reins of a terrible power had fallen. He was physically, morally, and intellectually third-rate. Acts of physical violence sickened him, but he could regard them with equanimity when performed by the sadists of his concentration camps 'for the future glory

Lutze, who betrayed Röhm

of the Reich'. Heydrich, on the other hand, was highly intelligent, a sado-masochist brimming with hatred for his own corrupted blood and screening that hatred behind denial and bitter anti-Semitism. In him, Heinrich Himmler observed with envy the strengths he lacked himself; and in Himmler, Reinhard Tristan Eugen Heydrich saw the archetypal weakling who symbolized the material most malleable to the touch of power. There was no doubt that Heydrich was a very dangerous man.

Even Hitler himself was not outside the realm of danger from his sorcerer's apprentice. True, he could at any time have wielded his power of blackmail over Heydrich; that had been the point of Himmler's assurance that Heydrich would 'always be grateful that we have overlooked . . . his impurity . . . [and] can at any time force him into submission by threats of disclosure'. But blackmail was in

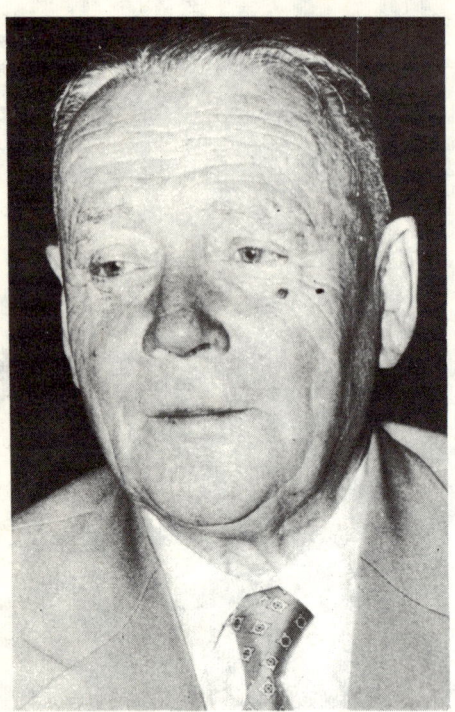

this case a two-edged sword. Hitler did not doubt that there existed a dossier stuffed with the more unsavoury details of his own life: his impotence, his syphilis, his coprophilia and the mysterious circumstances of the death of his niece and lover, Geli Raubal. And since it is axiomatic that the greater the heights of power achieved the greater the fall from grace will be, the Führer had good reason to regard Heydrich as a potential enemy. (He was right about the dossier: it fell into Himmler's hands after Heydrich's death and was shown to Felix Kersten, Himmler's physiotherapist, who was the first to

Left: **Conrad Patzig.** *Below left:* **Marshal Joseph Pilsudski.** *Below:* **Admiral Scheer**

reveal that Hitler was a syphilitic.) But Heydrich's talents as a ruthless organizer of suppression, murder, and other manifestations of totalitarianism made him too valuable to be discarded. So each was in the grip of the other.

With the direction of the SS, the weakened SA, the civil police and the Gestapo wholly in his grasp, Heydrich 'at once set about the Nazification of the entire German police organization', says his biographer Charles Wighton. 'In instructions to his subordinates he emphasized that National Socialism would only be successful historically when the National Socialist idea had been accepted by the entire German people by victory over the enemies of the State. That victory would only be assured when the enemy had been rendered completely unfit for any further action.

'To attain this end Heydrich bluntly announced that the police must abandon all "liberal principles" which had hitherto governed German police operations. The enemies were now the Jews, the Communists, the Freemasons' lodges and political churchmen. Against these he would throw all the police and secret service forces of the Nazi authoritarian state which were under his personal command. The Gestapo's task, he announced, would be to uncover and overcome all efforts throughout the entire Reich dangerous to the Nazi régime.'

Despite the immense range of his powers, however, there was a corner of the net that Heydrich did not have in his grasp; a corner that he would

have loved to control since it was an undercover organization of the kind so dear to his heart. This was the *Abwehr*, the Armed Forces High Command Intelligence Service which Canaris has served as a spy and schemer in the days of Heydrich's naval service.

The *Abwehr's* particular field was the normal one of any armed forces intelligence organization reporting via a Ministry to its Government: the establishment of a spy ring to ferret out the military activities of other countries, and (less normal outside totalitarian régimes) the appointment of foreign agents 'to combat ideological enemies outside the State'. It was commanded by a young naval captain, Konrad Patzig, whom Heydrich suspected – rightly – of knowing far too much about his past and ancestry and of resenting the power the former junior signals officer had acquired and still lusted to increase. With Patzig out of the way it might be easier to gain control of the *Abwehr* and thereby complete his command of every intelligence, security and police organization in the Reich.

It was not, for Heydrich, a difficult task. The 'round table' obliged with a useful snippet of information about Patzig's career. In 1932 he had ordered an aerial photo-reconnaissance of Poland's military defences and had received an official reprimand for doing so, since at the time there was in force an *entente cordiale* between Germany and her eastern neighbour. Marshal Pilsudski, Poland's *eminence grise*, had reasonably enough threatened to make an international incident of the affair and, equally reasonably, Patzig had had the reprimand entered in his records. Heydrich quite easily persuaded Hitler, to whom he now had easy access (which was always denied to Himmler, grovel as he might) that Patzig would serve the Reich much better if he were transferred to the active command of the *Admiral Scheer*, which transfer was made without further ado, leaving the coveted post of head of the *Abwehr* within Heydrich's grasp.

In the event, however, it eluded him – as it had eluded Himmler, one of whose objects in building up the SS had been to become in addition master of the High Command espionage network. Himmler's aim, however, had never been particularly direct or determined: he had only rather vaguely imagined the entire organized forces of the Reich falling ripely into his garden of Nazi ideology. Heydrich's purpose was much more resolute: it would extend the power he now wielded in civil and political matters into the *Wehrmacht* and thence into international espionage – a realm that could hardly have been more coveted by a man so beset by the urge to be involved in sinister machinations.

But there were others – not many – who could play the fox on an equal footing with Heydrich: notably Admiral Erich Raeder (as he now was), who had by no means forgotten the cavalier way in which Heydrich had refused his order to marry Otto Schlueter's daughter. Since now, at the end of 1934, Raeder was commander-in-chief of the rapidly, if secretly, expanding German navy, he was not without influence. On 24th September he had received a report, from his commander-in-chief of potential ships of the line, concerning an officer recommended for promotion. The report was in glowing terms and suggested that the officer would be equally suitable as Inspector General of the Navy, Deputy Admiral at a naval station, or Chief of the *Abwehr* in the Reich Ministry – 'the post that has recently fallen vacant as a result of the transfer of Captain Konrad Patzig to command of a ship of the line'.

Raeder had little hesitation in endorsing the recommendations; and on 1st January 1935 Captain Wilhelm Canaris took up his appointment as Chief of the *Abwehr*.

Entrance to Berlin Police Headquarters

At eight o'clock that morning, according to Ladislas Farago in *The Game of the Foxes*, 'the outgoing and incoming *Abwehr* chiefs settled down to a chatty conference. Patzig made no secret of his glee at leaving for greener pastures as skipper of the *Admiral Scheer*. He spoke feelingly about his problems, embroiled as he was in a bitter feud with Heinrich Himmler's internal security agency, the powerful *Reichssicherheitshauptamt*. He regaled his successor with embarrassing and painful incidents in Himmler's design on the *Abwehr*, and described the subtle but determined rivalry of young Nazi Reinhard Heydrich, chief of the *Sicherheitsdienst* or security service charged with political espionage.

'Patzig now told Canaris bluntly: "I am sorry for you, Captain, because you don't seem to realize what a mess you're getting into".

' "Please don't worry about me, Captain Patzig", Canaris said with a faint smile. "I'm an incurable optimist. And as far as those fellows are concerned, I think I know how to get along with them".

'Patzig stiffened and then said quietly: "If that is what you think, Captain Canaris, then I am sorry to say that this day is the beginning of your end".'

A gloomy prophecy not, in the end, mistaken. Canaris was condemned to death on 9th April 1945 by an SS court for his part in the conspiracy against Hitler. His aid to the conspirators amounted to virtually nothing; but after Heydrich's assassination Himmler carried on the personal vendetta against the *Abwehr* his henchman had pursued because he had failed to gain control of it, and Canaris and several other high ranking *Abwehr* men were mercilessly hunted down by the Gestapo until enough 'evidence' was assembled to ensure their execution.

Not that any enmity between Heydrich and his mentor was obvious on

Gestapo Headquarters

the renewal of their acquaintance early in 1935. Canaris was quickly promoted to Admiral, a rank in keeping with his appointment as head of the High Command Intelligence service, and he and his sometime protégé could now meet on terms of equality. Canaris did in fact know 'how to get along with those people' and the first thing he did was to pay a social call on the Heydrich family. There were now two children, both boys and good looking in the same way that their father had been before he was old enough for the evil behind the mask to glint through, and Canaris seemed to set great store by Lina Heydrich's advice to rent an empty house a few yards up the street in the Berlin suburb of Sudende. By June 1935 he and his wife had moved in and *soirees musicale* echoed the days at Kiel when Heydrich had forsaken music and attached himself to an enterprise offering considerably more scope for the urge to power that possessed him.

There were other social engagements besides Frau Canaris's chamber music evenings. 'When Captain Canaris appeared on the scene', Farago says, 'all of a sudden the moribund *Abwehr* came to life. He went to work with energy and brisk spirit . . . [and] organized convivial dinners for the entertainment of Heydrich and his staff in what he called *Kamaradschaftsabende*, evenings of comradeship. They were held regularly in a private room in the restaurant in the House of Flyers on Prinz Albrecht Strasse, next door to the grim Gestapo building where Heydrich had his office. This seemingly one-sided accommodation with Heydrich was of shrewd design and not necessarily a reflection of Canaris's true sentiments. While he was mending his fences he placated the Nazis mainly to develop the *Abwehr* according to his own ambitious plans.'

On the other side of the fences Canaris was so assiduously mending Heydrich was planning similarly to develop his own ambitious plans.

War

Hitler's first attempt to display his growing strength in terms of actual conquest was a botched-up job. His design was to accomplish what he called a 'reunion' of Austria with Germany, and to that end he built up the Austrian Nazi party as a Fifth Column whose acts of violence and terrorism were intended to achieve their climax in the murder of the Austrian Chancellor, Dr Engelbert Dolfuss, and the immediately conse-

quent seizure of power. The murder was committed easily enough. Heydrich provided a party of SS in Austrian army uniforms to close in on the Federal Chancellery at noon on 25th July 1934. Undetected by the police and sentries on duty until it was too late, they invaded the Chancellery and shot Dolfuss as he sat at his desk – though not very effectively, for it took him six hours to die. The next step as planned was to seize Radio Vienna and announce the downfall of Dolfuss at the hands of 'rebels who in all justice demand to see their country united with the German Reich'. But the SS men were in general inept, not only as killers; and there were too many of them – specifically 154. They crowded the corridors of the Chancellery and were easily rounded up by troops hastily summoned by the tele-

Funeral of Dr Dolfuss

phone they had failed to cut off.

The attempt to pull Austria into the Reich having failed, Hitler proclaimed that he was shocked at the 'cruel murder of Dr Dolfuss by Austrian terrorists' and sent an emissary in the person of Franz von Papen to Vienna to 'restore normal and friendly relations' with the new Chancellor, Kurt von Schuschnigg. His crocodile tears flooded the more gullible sections of the foreign press – the London *Times* and *Daily Mail* and the Paris *Le Matin* particularly – and for a long time obscured his new plans for the *Ansschluss*, which was of course exactly what he intended. Wisely, he realized that both his military and diplomatic strengths were inadequate to force the venture; and during the years spent on increasing them, Himmler and Heydrich were told to make way for the second attempt. It was an operation given the name 'Otto'; it could have been called Trojan Horse, for it involved the sort of tactics one would expect to hide behind – or inside – such a name. No-one could have been more efficient at this new Fifth Column enterprise than Heydrich who, using as tools the Gestapo and SD (and, as a number one henchman, Walter Schellenberg) soon established sources of information inside the Austrian Chancellery that led to a list of countless 'suspects' who were to be the justification for eventual military action.

Before the plans for that action were completed Hitler flourished his enormously expanded forces in the occupation of the Rhineland (several years in advance of the date stipulated by the Versailles Treaty and confirmed by the Locarno Pact) which had been a demilitarized zone since 1930. On 7th March 1936 his troops marched across the Rhine bridges and waited for the French to show some sign of fight. They did nothing but reinforce the Maginot Line and appeal to Britain to support them in accordance with the terms of the Locarno Treaty. Not for the first, or last, time Britain wobbled at the possibility of war. Her Foreign Secretary, Anthony Eden, made a flaccid speech in parliament two days later which admitted that Hitler's *coup* made nonsense of the principle of treaties but revealed 'no reason to suppose that Germany's present action threatens hostilities' – in witness of which he could later (on 30th March) point to the overwhelming approval the German citizenry had given in a referendum asking whether or not they approved of the 'restoration' of their 'beloved Rhineland'. The 98.8 favourable vote was understandable when one thinks of Heydrich's Gestapo minions clouding the issue with unspoken but nonetheless implicit threats of concentration camps for those who voted *Nein*. Why the favourable reception of Hitler's *coup* in Germany should have signified non-threatening intentions he did not make clear – possibly because it was beyond his wit to do so.

Hitler was later to say (as recorded by his interpreter, Paul Schmidt):

'The forty-eight hours after the march into the Rhineland were the most nerve-wracking in my life. If the French had then marched into the Rhineland with British support, we would have had to withdraw with our tails between our legs, for the military forces at our disposal amounted to only four brigades and would have been wholly inadequate for even a moderate resistance'.

The quavering diplomacy of France and Britain having met his bluff with all the strength of a blancmange, he now put out as many olive branches as an octopus might have waved: non-aggression pacts with Belgium and France; an invitation to Britain and Italy to guarantee the Belgian and French frontiers; the immediate demilitarization of both sides of the Franco-German border (which ploy, no-one seems to have realized, would have meant the evacuation of the Maginot Line, in which France kept a

Von Papen leaves for Vienna as Ambassador to Austria

Germany reoccupies the Rhineland

Symbolic removal of the Austrian frontier during the Anschluss, 1938

pathetic but quite unjustified faith); and a renewal of the non-aggression pacts with Poland and Czechoslovakia. Thus the potentially explosive European situation was on the face of it smoothed over until, with Mussolini's invasion of Abyssinia and Hitler's deliberately challenging declaration that Germany was rearming and tearing to shreds the remaining rags of the Versailles Treaty as well as seceding from the League of Nations, it became clear that the cracks in the European edifice could no longer be papered over with conciliatory gestures from Britain. Nevertheless conciliation was the keynote of her diplomacy up to and beyond the Munich pact of 1938.

By then Austria was in Hitler's hands. Heydrich had organized the events leading up to the annexation with typical expertise. With Schellenberg's help he had contrived the infiltration of self-seeking Nazis into Schuschnigg's Chancellery. They included two Austrian lawyers, Ernst Kaltenbrunner and Artur Seyss-Inquart, and a mongrel lout called Odilo Globocnik. Another, who was extremely helpful in assembling suitable dossiers of information on the Jews who accounted for a large proportion of the Austrian population, particularly in Vienna, was one Karl Adolf Eichmann.

'In every direction the Jews will prove stumbling blocks', Heydrich told him at a meeting called and recorded by Hitler. 'There will be a special section of the SD to cope with the menace, and that will be your concern'.

Then and there the euphemistically entitled 'Office for Jewish Emigration' was established and remained Eichmann's concern until the end. It efficiently organized the extermination of six million Jews.

There was no doubt about the

Nazi troops ride into Salzburg

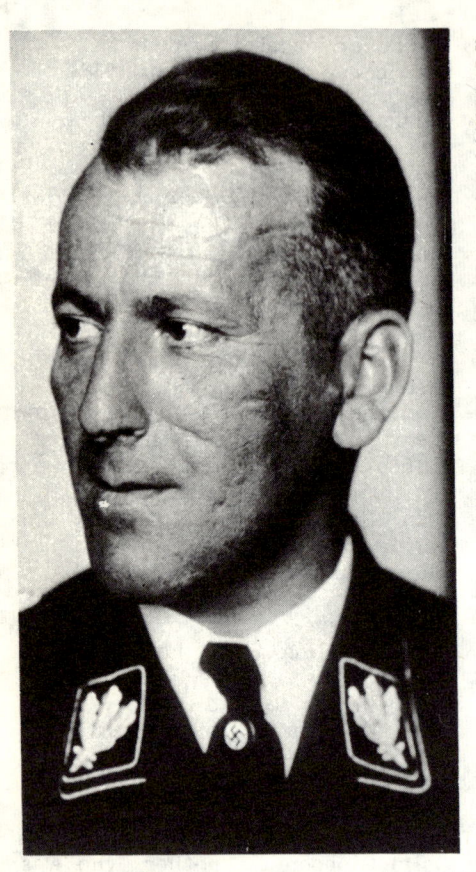

success of the *Anschluss* this time. Thanks to Heydrich's Trojan Horse the Schuschnigg government collapsed on 11th March 1938 and Seyss-Inquart and Kaltenbrunner became Chancellor and Minister of the Interior respectively. Schuschnigg and the President, Wilhelm Miklas, were arrested along with all potential opponents of Nazism 'pending a free plebiscite in which the Austrian people will vote for or against the union of their country with Greater Germany'.

Those who voted against the *Anschluss* amounted to 0.25 per cent of the population. The other 99.75 per cent were only too well aware of the probable consequences if they didn't set their *Ja* to the ballot paper. William Shirer says:

'In the polling station which I visited in Vienna that Sunday afternoon, wide slits in the corner of the polling booths gave the Nazi election committee sitting a few feet away a

Left: Ernst Kaltenbrunner. *Below:* Konrad Henlein. *Right:* Dr Seyss-Inquart *Far right:* Adolf Eichmann. *Below right:* Globocnik. *Below far right:* Theodor Eicke, Commandant of Dachau

good view of how one voted. In the country districts few bothered – or dared – to cast their ballots in the secrecy of the booth, they voted openly for all to see'.

The annexation had been virtually bloodless. The army and the air force, though ominously present in huge numbers, were not called upon to fire a shot or drop a bomb. The SS had prepared the way too well for force to be necessary.

The plebiscite accomplished, Himmler appointed Heydrich to the command of all police and security forces in Austria, which for a while was renamed Ostmark and subsequently became an unnamed division of the new Greater Germany.

'Austria', Heydrich wrote in the SS Journal *Das Schwarze Korps*, 'is now an area where the will of the Führer can be carried out as a result of the successful conclusion of the bitter fight against all political, spiritual and criminal elements who opposed the idea of a single German people. The former Austrian police were responsible for the deaths of a large number of good fanatical Germans. The honour of the force was rescued only by the National Socialist policemen who gave their lives and freedom for the dream of a Greater Germany.' The carrying out of the will of the Führer meant in practice a wave of mass terrorism in which Kaltenbrunner and Globocnik were given a mandate to persecute. The victims of their violence were of course all opponents of the Nazi régime, whether suspected or proven, particularly the Jews. Shirer again:

'For the first few weeks the behaviour of the Vienna Nazis was worse than anything I had seen in Germany. There was an orgy of sadism. Day after day large numbers of Jewish men and women could be seen scrubbing Schuschnigg signs off the sidewalk and cleaning the gutters. While they worked on their hands and knees with jeering storm troopers standing over them, crowds gathered to taunt them. Hundreds of Jews, men and women, were picked off the streets and put to work cleaning public latrines and toilets of the barracks where the SA and SS were quartered. Tens of thousands more were jailed. Their worldly possessions were confiscated or stolen. I myself, from our apartment in the Plosslgasse, watched squads of SS men carting off silver, tapestries, paintings and other loot from the Rothschild palace next door. Baron Louis de Rothschild himself was later able to buy his way out of Vienna by turning over his steel mills to the Hermann Göring works. Perhaps half of the city's 180,000 Jews managed, by the time the war started, to purchase their freedom to emigrate by handing over what they owned to the Nazis.'

On Heydrich's personal order Schuschnigg was arrested and confined in an attic room of the Metropole Hotel, Vienna. He was 'to be given the honour of attending personally upon the SS on duty in the hotel'. That meant that he had to clean their quarters, empty their slops, run their errands from one part of the hotel to another, and make obeisances to them each time he was summoned. Eighteen months later – also on Heydrich's order – he was transferred to Dachau concentration camp with his wife. The departure of the 'special train' of two cattle trucks that took him and 200 other 'proven opponents' of the régime was watched by Heydrich, who had flown from Berlin specially to be entertained by the spectacle. He and Himmler sat in the back of their official car, which had been driven into the siding from which the train would depart and watched the entraining of the prisoners. It was the evening of Sunday 3rd September 1939. The lorries with their hapless cargo backed down to the loading bay. It was dusk and two machine-gun posts were set up in case there should be any attempts at escape. When the gunners were in position the doors of the first lorry were opened and the prisoners herded down the ramp and into the cattle trucks. Their shuffling passage was aided by the rifle butts of the SS guards. A signal gantry crossed the sidings and red and green lights glinted through the rising smoke from locomotives; and the hissing of steam mingled with the shouts of the guards and the cries of those who were being beaten or kicked into the cattle trucks. They were trucks with slatted sides, and, as they filled up, the faces of the condemned could be seen like the death-masks of ancient warriors peering through the interstices of time.

Heydrich watched the spectacle impassively. Himmler recorded afterward that he made only one comment: 'It is like watching the animals being driven into the ark'. Though understandably he doesn't mention it, it is probable that Himmler, sickened always by the sight of violence, though never by its commission, shrank back in the seat beside his henchman.

The relationship between these two was a curious one. 'Blood brothers in the art of cruelty' they were called by Schuschnigg in his book *Austrian Requiem*. That, certainly; but they were also *ego* and *alter ego*, virulently jealous of each other's power yet dependent on each other for it. Heydrich's own schizophrenic condition, reflected in his self-hatred, was echoed in the concealed hostility he felt toward Himmler's mad ideological notions, dim wits, and weakness of spirit. Himmler's continual adulation of Heydrich in diaries and journals was the visible proof that the younger man had nothing to fear from him. He saw himself as being in masterly control of everything from the reconstitution of the great Aryan race to the smallest detail of office routine; he was certainly cunning enough to suppress any evidence, visible or audible, that might be used against him. Though treachery formed no part of his character and he had in fact nothing to conceal but his own significance outside Nazi politics he had no doubt that there was, somewhere, a Himmler dossier in which were recorded a thousand chance remarks or trivial acts; nor had he any doubts as to the interpretations that could be woven into such records. Who should know better than the man who had taken the first step toward the formation of the Gestapo? Hence the safeguard of adulation and co-operation. His fears remained suppressed, his pale eyes expressionless behind *pincenez*. But they concealed the envy he felt of his dashing *alter ego* – Heydrich, whose abilities he had nurtured and which were now interlocked with his own. To be sure, clashes between them were rare and invariably silent, amounting to no more than the equivalent of an electrical impulse bridging the gap between two opposing poles; and doubtless one such flash of emnity passed between them that night of 3rd September 1939 as they watched the departure of the train for Dachau; for Heydrich had engineered the opening gambit of the war. But Himmler, playing safe, had recorded his 'utmost admiration' for Heydrich's skill in carrying out 'the Führer's plans for world future'.

The Führer's plans for world future, in opposition to which Britain and France had offered little but rumbling noises of disapproval, had been spinning ahead with great success since the Austrian *Anschluss*. Their motive power was provided in a Top Secret directive dated 24th July 1937 which, after stating categorically that 'neither Russia nor the Western Powers have any desire for war', went on to say that even so preparations must be made to exploit 'politically favourable opportunities should they occur; for the aim of German policy is to make secure and enlarge the German racial community. It is therefore a question of space [*Lebensraum*], for the German peoples have a right to greater living space than other nations.' The claim having been staked, the method of enforcing it was discussed:

'An extension to the East can begin with a surprise German operation against Czechoslovakia in order to parry the imminent attack of a superior enemy coalition. The necessary conditions to justify such an action politically and in the eyes of international law must be created *beforehand*.' Conveniently, the Sudeten Germans were at hand to provide the 'justification'. These were German nationals, rather more than three million of them, who since 1934 had been led by one Konrad Henlein, Hitler's minion, and of course financed by the Nazi party. It was another Trojan Horse operation, in a country that was particularly vulnerable to such machinations; for the republic, created after the First World War, was one in which dissident minorities were continually demanding impractical measures of autonomy. Bohemians, Moravians, Czechs, Slovaks, Ruthenians and Hungarians lived in uneasy peace; and the presence of the 'Sudeten' Germans (who were in fact Austrians) did nothing to help the situation. With Henlein's leadership, however, they did an enormous amount to help Hitler in his declared policy of eastward expansion. Their continual cry was for the establishment of an independent totalitarian state within the democratic Czechoslovak republic – an object clearly unacceptable to the government, for though the peace of these mingled nationals was an uneasy one they at least had full civil and voting rights and all were represented in the central government.

Any threat of attack on Czechoslovakia by Germany was, in the terms of the peace treaties, to be met by France, Britain and Russia. But when, early in September 1938, the threat actually materialized and German troops began to mass on the Czechoslovakian border, Britain and France both backed down. There might well have been an element of bluff in Hitler's demands, as there had been two years earlier in his occupation of the Rhineland; but this time he was bluffing, if at all, from a position of strength. Britain's unpreparedness, a consequence of her peace-at-any-price policy, was a key factor in the situation. Czechoslovakia was told that she must either yield to Hitler's demands or fight alone. Prime Ministers Chamberlain and Daladier, trembling with their eagerness to avert war, allowed no more than a token mobilization of the British fleet. On 28th September they sped to Munich, whither they had been summoned by a snap of Hitler's fingers (euphemistically called an 'invitation') to 'settle the matter' with the Führer and Mussolini. That was the infamous 'Peace in Our Time' conference and the result of it was complete agreement to accept Hitler's demands for the occupation of the Sudetenland within the next two weeks, plus the illusory relief of the Munich 'scrap of paper'. Immediately, the democratic government fell to pieces; the President, Eduard Benes, fled into exile in America, and a single-party government was formed and backed by an Enabling Act that effectively abolished all democratic rights and substituted rule by decree. Yet another step in 'the Führer's plans for world future' had been successfully taken.

Heydrich had had little to do with the annexation and dismemberment of the Czechoslovakian republic. But his activities during the crisis autumn of 1938 had much to do with his appointment as 'Protector' of the newly named State of Bohemia-Moravia. (That was to come in September 1941.) For if Hitler had needed any further proof of Heydrich's ability as an administrator and manufacturer of events suitable for all purposes he would have found it in the affair of Ernst von Rath and Herschel Grynspan.

Ernst von Rath worked in a minor secretarial position in the German

Chamberlain arrives in Munich

Embassy in Paris. He was young and foolish enough to have made critical remarks about Nazi policy. These, naturally, had fallen upon the ears of one of Heydrich's *Leute* informers and had made their way up the spiral to the stage where he had become a Gestapo suspect. That was merely routine. The Gestapo chief, Heinrich Müller, had stuck a red tab on the dossier relating to Rath, which meant that it came before him once a month to enable him to study additional information. When the time came the red tab would be superseded by a blue one and it would be time to strike. For the moment, the rope was being paid out and in due course, it was supposed, he would hang himself. And no doubt the supposition was a reasonable one. But it was overtaken by events. Chief among them was an expulsion order covering the deportation of 23,000 Polish Jews from Germany – an order that had been issued by Heydrich wearing his SD hat at the beginning of September 1938. Poland, however, refused to accept them and they were trapped in a narrow strip of land along the German-Polish border, homeless, surrounded with what they had been able to rescue of their possessions, and living in encampments contrived from no more than they were able to provide from the bleak border country.

It was a familiar situation to a race that for centuries had been driven from one land to another. But familiarity in no sense alleviated the distress that fell upon them as the first icy winds of winter blew across the plain from the east. Foraging for themselves in country where the few occupants were fearful of trapping themselves in networks of alleged treachery, they daily fared more disastrously.

One of the families thus facing the terrible hazards of winter and starvation was named Grynspan. Their son,

Rath's murderer Herschel Grynspan, led away by police

Ernest von Rath

Herschel, had escaped the deportation order because he was at that time living with an uncle in Paris. But the news of their plight had not escaped him. He was seventeen years old and rather neurotic by temperament and during a period of wretchedness brought about by a despairing letter he had received from friends of the family decided to murder the German Ambassador in Paris, Count Johannes von Welczek. With this otherwise unplanned object he went to the Embassy and simply asked the receptionist for an interview with the Ambassador. Naturally enquiry was made as to his business, and when he refused to answer and began to behave rather oddly, shivering as if with fever and talking rapidly but without much coherence, the receptionist rang for assistance from the inner office.

The call was answered by Rath after a slight delay. He came into the entrance hall of the Embassy to meet the six wildly aimed bullets from

Count Johannes von Welczek, German Ambassador in Paris

Grynspan's revolver. Three of these did no damage at all beyond shattering an elaborate mirror on the wall and embedding themselves in the panelling behind the receptionist's desk; the other three pierced Rath's foot, shoulder and stomach. Two days later he died in hospital.

Had he known of the alternative fate that awaited him he might well have been thankful; for only the previous week, on 5th November, Müller had observed that additional information had come to hand relating to Rath's foolishly spoken comments on Nazi policy and a blue seal had been stuck on his dossier. After arrest by the Gestapo he would undoubtedly have been sent to a concentration camp for 'infidelity' intolerable in a diplomat. He did well to die in the comfort of a hospital bed with hastily summoned relations at his side.

His death was of supreme unimportance to the Nazi machine. He was an extremely minor cog whose removal would have not the slightest effect on its working. But on the Nazi image . . . That was another matter altogether. Heydrich saw and seized its possibilities immediately.

Grynspan's fate was never determined – anyway not publicly. He was arrested as he ran from the Embassy, but no publicity was ever given to his trial or the outcome of it. And that was less than astonishing, for as an isolated news item it would have been of little use. As an excuse, however, for a much greater revenge for the assassination of a German representative of the Nazi régime in a foreign country – and an assassination, moreover, deliberately carried out by a Jew – it was most valuable.

On the night of 9th November Heydrich ordered that 'spontaneous demonstrations' were to be organized throughout Germany against the Jews for their murder of Rath – 'since

Synagogues are burned in reprisal

they are collectively responsible for the violent act of one of their race'. It was a first-rate chance to demonstrate the efficiency of his organizations. Within an hour SS, Gestapo and Party leaders had met and discussed practical measures to organize the 'spontaneous' demonstrations. In the early hours of the morning they received by teleprinter Heydrich's instructions for the conduct of the demonstrations:

'1. Only such measures are to be taken which do not involve danger to German life or property. For instance, synagogues are to be burnt down only when there is no danger of fire to the surroundings.

'2. Business and private apartments of Jews may be destroyed but not looted.

'3. The demonstrations which are going to take place must not be hindered by the civil police.

'4. As many Jews, especially rich ones, are to be arrested as can be accommodated in the existing prisons. Upon their arrest the appropriate concentration camps should be contacted immediately, in order to confine them in these camps as soon as possible.'

Two days later he was able to send a preliminary report to Hitler:

'The extent of the destruction of Jewish shops and houses cannot yet be verified by figures. The 815 shops and 171 dwelling houses that have been set on fire indicate only a small percentage of the actual damage by arson. Certainly there were 200 synagogues destroyed by fire and the number of Jews so far arrested is 20,000. There may be some complications over insurance claims, many of the Jewish shops being in buildings that are owned by non-Jews. It was of course impossible to curb the enthusiasm of the people for their spontaneous demonstration and therefore little discrimination was exercised. I have seen the *Reichsmarshal* [Göring] and we are agreed that the best course to follow would be for the insurance companies to settle the Jews' claim in full and then to confiscate the money and return it to the insurers. My information is that claims for broken glass alone would amount to some five million marks and the glass would have to be imported against foreign exchange, of which we are extremely short. As for the practical matter of clearing up the destruction, this is being arranged by releasing Jews in gangs from the concentration camps and having them clear up their own messes under supervision. The courts will impose upon them a fine of a billion marks and this will be paid out of the proceeds of their confiscated property. Heil Hitler!'

The pogrom that began with 'The Night of Broken Glass' and was to have no end during the lifetime of the Third Reich was seen by Hitler to be a triumph of cunning and organisation on Heydrich's part. It is clear from remarks recorded in his *Table Talk* that he had great things in mind for the man he called 'The genius of all the police and security forces of the Reich'. A hint was dropped that Heydrich would soon be appointed 'Protector' of the dismembered republic of Czechoslovakia now known as Bohemia-Moravia and there be given a chance to show his mettle as administrator of an entire satellite state. The job would be done temporarily by Baron von Neurath, an old aristocrat who had been Foreign Minister and, earlier, Ambassador to the Court of St James in London, but who was now declining in health and ability and could be expected to muddle things, thus providing the opportunity for the Führer to give him his *congé*. All that would be seen to in due course. 'For the time being', Himmler wrote, 'Heydrich is too busy carrying out the Führer's wishes, and my plans, for the elimination of the blood of Jewry from the German nation'.

He was also busy with more amusing, but in their way no less important, matters. His undiminished sexual promiscuity had combined with his professional eagerness to further the causes of Nazism by establishing a VIP brothel in Berlin. It was called Salon Kitty and was situated well away from the red-light district so that the utmost discretion could be offered to those tempted to use it. The users, of course, were all carefully selected not for any benefit they could confer on themselves by brief associations with the girls there, but for the benefits they could shower on the SD and Gestapo by their temporarily unbuttoned lips. They were Nazis on whom some suspicion had settled for one reason or another, foreign diplomats, press men, and the pleasure-seeking faithful of the Party – including, needless to say, Heydrich himself. They were nursed in luxurious surroundings and invited to meet some of the most beautiful girls in Germany (who were also some of the most beautiful girls in the pay of the Gestapo). The playthings of the Salon Kitty naturally included every imaginable erotic device and many that were almost unimaginable. They also included monitoring and recording devices, two-way mirrors (other than those intended for the use of voyeur customers), hidden cameras and similar machinery that in the normal traditions of hospitality a guest would be unlikely to expect in his host's house.

The staff who, from the Madam down the scale to the sweepers and scrubbers, were entirely in the pay of the Gestapo or SD, had been recruited by one of Heydrich's most efficient henchmen, Alfred Naujocks. Naujocks was an underworld creature who had been found by Heydrich working in one of the Kurfurstendam night clubs as a waiter. He had a degree in engineering awarded by Kiel University but preferred the seedier life of backstreet intrigue in which he could make far more money and at the same time indulge his liking for both brutality and blackmail. He had joined the SS in 1931 and Heydrich had been surprised when, himself in SS uniform, he had been approached by Naujocks by way of a sentence written on the bill Heydrich had just been presented with in the night club he was at the time frequenting:

'*Herr Obergruppenführer!* I request privilege of talk with you and request for special assignment'.

This was followed by his SS number and name. The message appealed to Heydrich because of its cloak-and-dagger style and as a result of the subsequent interview he put Naujocks on special duties in the SD. He had turned out to be a most efficient contributor of information, was useful in the more heavy-handed departments of thuggery and murder when required, and had been proved by the internal evidence of the 'round table' and the cross-references of countless *Leute* to be thoroughly reliable. (He was the man who in the early stages of the war proposed and planned the operation to undermine the British economy by printing thousands of forged banknotes and dropping them over Britain.) In many minor operations he served as Heydrich's right-hand man; and when Salon Kitty came to be planned he contrived all its secret mechanisms and staffed it with girls who were not only beautiful but whose security rating was the highest attainable. Their pay was no trifle either, judging from the salary bill, which was 150,000 marks a week and was paid from Party funds. It was here that Hitler came when in Berlin to indulge his perversion of coprophilia, and photographs of him dabbling in excreta and observing, with all the excitement of a physicist concluding an experiment, girls urinating are said to have existed in the collection of Heinrich Hoffmann, his photographer. (Presumably he riffled through them to experience masturbatory titillation when too busy for actual indulgence.)

Heydrich, who could so effectively organize concentration camps, a pogrom such as 'The Night of the Broken Glass', and a useful Intelligence centre disguised as a brothel, was, to Hitler's mind, to be fully trusted. That he could operate matters at international level had been proved by the Trojan Horse affair in Austria. 'If it comes to war', Hitler is recorded in *Table Talk* as saying, 'I know exactly whom I will entrust the opening gambit to.'

The opening gambit was, officially, Hitler's notorious Directive No. 1 for the Conduct of the War, dated 31st August 1939:

'1. Now all the political possibilities of disposing by peaceful means of a situation on the Eastern Frontier which is intolerable for Germany are exhausted, I have determined on a solution by force.

'2. The attack on Poland is to be carried out in accordance with the preparations made, with the alterations which result, where the Army is concerned, from the fact that it has in the meantime almost completed its dispositions. Allotment of tasks and the operational target remain unchanged. Date of attack: 1st September 1939. Time of attack: 4.45am. This timing also applies to the operation at Gdynia, Bay of Danzig and the Dirschau Bridge.

'3. In the West it is important that the responsibility for the opening of hostilities should rest squarely on England and France.'

But it would be difficult to place responsibility for the opening of hostilities on the Allies without some kind of excuse for marching German troops across the border into Poland. Chamberlain, the British Prime Minister, Henderson, the British Ambassador in Berlin, and a number of well-meaning neutrals were busily flapping about like terrified hens and trying to preserve the last shreds of world peace. 'At least there must be on record,' Hitler said, 'if only for propaganda purposes, proof that we did not make the first move.' Heydrich, therefore, had been entrusted with concocting the 'evi-

dence'.

Two weeks before Directive No. 1 had been signed Heydrich had been playing croquet on the lawn of Canaris's home. There was to be some music in the evening and Schellenberg, who also was present, says that Heydrich had been compiling the programme with Erika Canaris and they had decided to conclude the evening with Haydn's Emperor Quartet.

'Between the end of the game and the evening cocktails we went into Canaris's study and Heydrich made what seemed to both Canaris and me a strange request. He wanted a good quantity – a hundred and fifty or so was the number he specified – of Polish army uniforms of assorted sizes. "For what purpose?" Canaris wanted to know. "For the Führer's purpose", Heydrich replied. Although on the face of it these two were still friendly there was an undercurrent of enmity that probably arose from Heydrich's having been unable to gain control of the *Abwehr*. Also, such fear as Canaris was capable of – he wasn't a chickenhearted man – was fed by the cold brutality and permanent menace behind the snake-like eyes of what he called "the cleverest brute of them all with his high intelligence and the secret self-hatred that turned him into the icy monster who was the

Kristallnacht, 1938. Jewish-owned property is attacked

main architect of the solution to the Jewish Problem". Nothing more was said about the uniforms, and it was pretty clear to me that Canaris was going to do a good deal of thinking and investigation before he did anything about supplying them.'

The matter, however, was taken out of Canaris's hands. Two days later, on 18th August, he received a direct order from Hitler to supply 'the uniforms and accessories as required for Upper Silesia in the context of Operation Himmler, which will be carried out at the proper time and of which you need know nothing more, since the *Abwehr* is not involved'.

Himmler's name had, one assumes, been given to the operation to propitiate him. He had recently crossed swords with Heydrich – not for the first time – over some nonsensical ideological notion. Heydrich had sneered contemptuously, Schellenberg tells us, 'and icily commented on Himmler's illogicality. The *Reichsführer* received the comment as if he'd been whipped. Then he snarled back, "You and your damned logic – your cold, brutal logic... it kills every idea in the world". You could have cut the atmosphere with a knife'. So no doubt some propitiatory gesture had to be made to Himmler. But if ever an undertaking should have been named for its planner it was the incident at the Gleiwitz radio station; for though Naujocks was the man who carried it through the plan was Heydrich's.

Gleiwitz is a town in Upper Silesia, a few miles from the Polish border. Its small booster radio station was linked with Radio Breslau on the German national network, and Heydrich's idea was to fake an attack on the station by 'Poles' who would overcome the staff, seize the transmitter, and broadcast a violently provocative diatribe that would justify an all-out attack on Poland. Naujocks himself outlined the plan at his trial in Nuremberg in 1945:

'On or about 10th August 1939 the chief of the SD, Heydrich, personally ordered me to simulate an attack on the radio station near Gleiwitz near the Polish border and to make it appear that the attacking force consisted of Poles. Heydrich said: "Practical proof is needed for these attacks of the Poles for the foreign press as well as for German propaganda".

'My instructions were to seize the radio station and to hold it long enough to permit a Polish-speaking German who would be put at my disposal to broadcast a speech in Polish. Heydrich told me that he would prepare the speech himself and that it would state that the time had come for conflict between Germans and Poles. He also told me that Germany would attack Poland as a consequence.

'I went to Gleiwitz and waited there fourteen days ... Between 25th and 31st August I went to see Heinrich Müller, head of the Gestapo, who was then near by at Oppeln. In my presence Müller discussed with a man named Mehlhorn plans for another border incident in which it should be made to appear that Polish soldiers were attacking German troops. Müller stated that he had a number of condemned criminals who were to be dressed in Polish uniforms and left dead on the ground at the scene of the incident to show they had been killed while attacking. For the purpose they were to be given fatal injections by a doctor employed by Heydrich. Then they were also to be given gunshot wounds. After the incident members of the press and other persons were to be taken to the spot.

'Müller told me he had an order from Heydrich to make one of these criminals available to me for the action at Gleiwitz. The code name by which he referred to these criminals was "Canned Goods".'

In the event it turned out to be a highly melodramatic performance, with cars screaming to a halt, bloodied-up bodies being dumped on the steps of the radio station, a last-minute panic because the radio engineer in the party of attackers could not find the right switch to link the broadcast with the national network, and unexpected armed resistance from the staff on duty – who, though naturally German Nazis – had to be sacrificed in the interests of credibility. One of the supposed Polish insurgents attacking – they were in fact all Polish speaking SS men wearing the uniforms and carrying the Polish small-arms provided reluctantly by Canaris – also was killed and had to be left among the injected bodies of the 'condemned

criminals' (these 'Canned Goods', as Müller called them, came from Eichmann's concentration camp at Dachau) who were supposed to have been shot by the heroic defenders of the station.

Though in minor respects the scheme misfired there was no doubt of its success as a whole. Goebbel's propaganda machinery switched into action with smooth efficiency and next morning every paper and every radio news bulletin headlined the 'Polish demand for conflict' and the 'unprovoked attack on German soil'.

Polish border barrier comes down

All the leading articles dealt gravely with 'this new issue of deliberate aggression at a moment when the Führer is fighting for a just form of world peace'. The inflammatory broadcast speech which Heydrich had so carefully composed was printed verbatim, and its key passage challenging Germany to conflict was met in the official Nazi paper *Völkischer Beobachter* with a pseudo dignified acceptance and an assurance that 'German troops are ready to march'. Which of course they were; and did so, into Poland, in accordance with the planned timing of Directive No 1, at 4.45am on Friday 1st September.

Heydrich's plan, blatantly contrived though it was, and seen as such by even the most gullible sections of the Allied press, had served its purpose. The war had begun. For months afterward Heydrich showed Italian and other diplomats a model of the Gleiwitz radio station and observed superciliously, 'That was where the war started'.

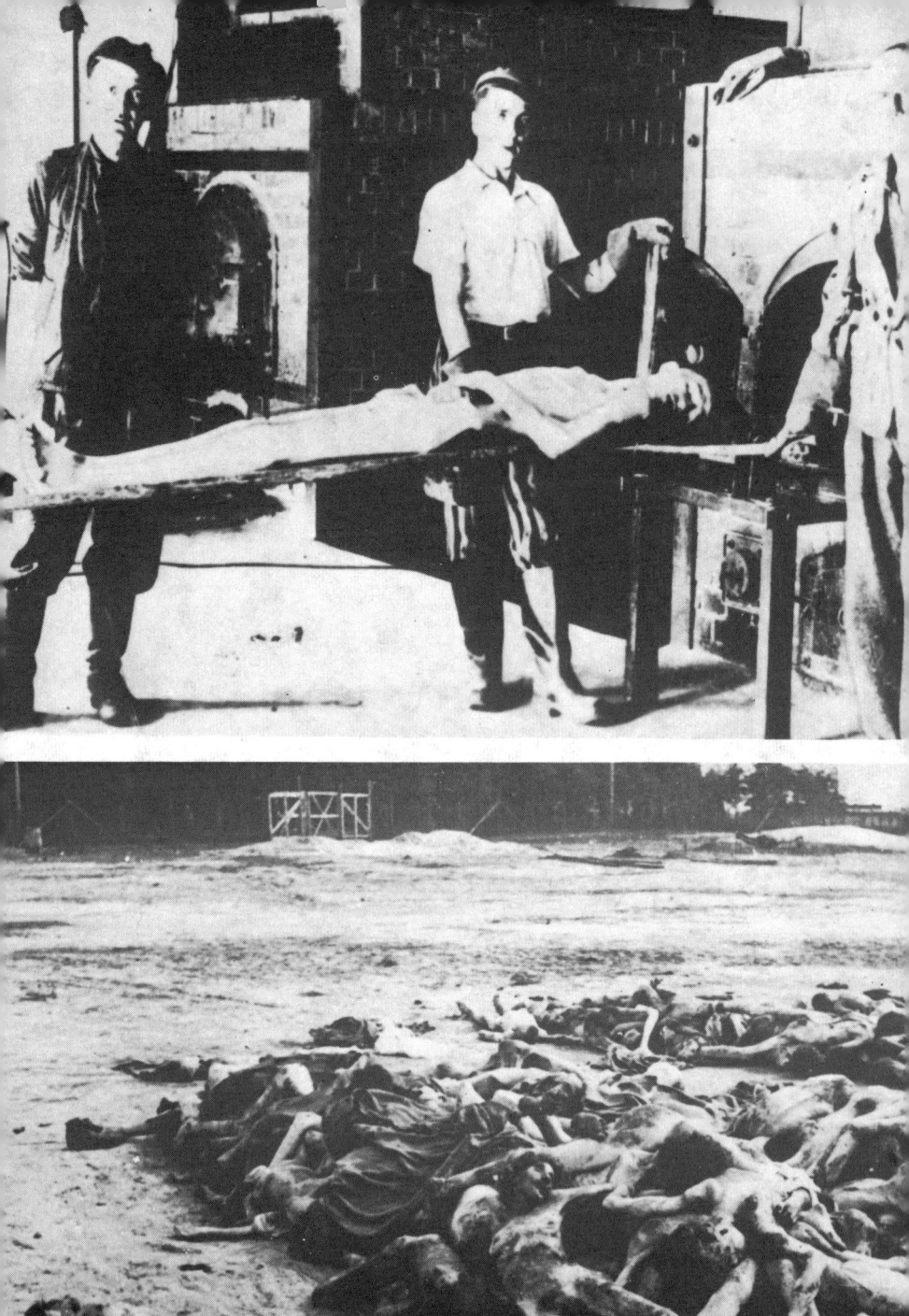

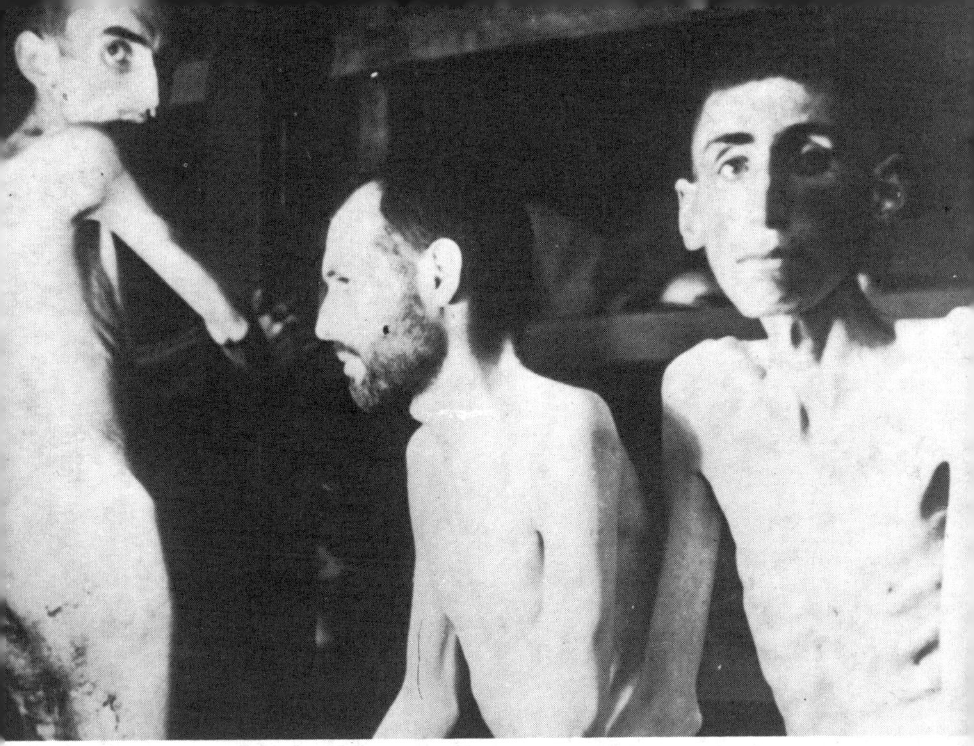

Above left, below left, above: Konzentrationslager – the victims. *Below:* Execution

Triumph

Poland was completely overrun by 17th September. Russian troops, eager for the carve-up Hitler had agreed with Stalin, pushed in from the east and the last shreds of resistance were broken by 4th October. Heydrich, restless for action other than of the administrative kind, drafted himself into the Luftwaffe and flew many sorties over the North Sea in a Me 110. He was the only top-rank Nazi to do so. His combat card recorded ninety-seven missions over England and France; and he was awarded the Iron Cross for his achievements as a fighter pilot.

Decorations, however, were of no interest to him. At this stage of his obsessional journey to personal power he was much more concerned to gain Hitler's approval for the project of joining into a single organisation the Gestapo, the *Reich Kripo* (roughly the equivalent of the British CID) and the SD. The super-organization, to be called the RHSA(*Reichssicherheithauptamv*) or Reich Chief Security Office, would give him complete control of every Intelligence, Secret Service and Secret Police organization in the Reich except the coveted *Abwehr*, which Canaris continued to guard jealously. The SS, now armed and part of the *Wehrmacht*, would remain Himmler's pride and joy; and as far as Heydrich was concerned he was welcome to it. The *Reichsführer*, fancying himself as an Army Commander – an occupation in which he was singularly useless – had provided himself with a special private train, *Sonderzug Heinrich*, in which he trailed about after Hitler, listening with amazement and adoration to Hitler's brilliant expositions of military strategy. While he listened, Walter Schellenberg, whom Heydrich had established aboard *Sonderzug Heinrich* as his personal spy, listened to Himmler and his various hangers-on (some of whom were less than pleased at the threat of Heydrich's increasing power) and fed back much useful information for Heydrich's files.

The formal establishment of the RSHA was accomplished on 27th September, the day after Hitler, satisfied that Poland was conquered, returned from the front. Klaus Schmidt, who had remained in desultory correspondence with Heydrich since their schools days, says:

'From the day of the creation of the RSHA Heydrich did what he liked for all practical purposes. He was officially subordinate to Himmler as *Reichsführer-SS*, but in practice he was supreme. He knew he was the motive power behind Himmler. And when each day he visited Himmler to discuss reports on the other leaders of the Third Reich and their policies, it was always Heydrich who decided what action should be taken — action which would either strengthen or weaken Himmler according to Heydrich's wish.'

There were other forms of action in which Heydrich took icy pleasure during the Polish campaign. He had been given authority by Hitler – signed and handed over on 5th October – 'To take immediate measures against the Polish Jews and at the same time undermine the influence of the priests of the Catholic church so that the Germanic peoples can have every opportunity to exploit the *lebensraum* they have gained in battle.'

'The house cleaning' as Heydrich called it 'will take special note not only of Jews [of whom there were three million in Poland] but also of the intelligentsia of whatever creed; the clergy of all denominations for their aptitude in misunderstanding the aim of the Third Reich, which is on a far higher plane than any religious doctrine; and the so-called nobility, who are so steeped in fanciful traditions that they can be more dangerous than their pettifogging little efforts at resistance lead one to believe. Concentration camps are to be erected with the utmost speed and all these useless and dangerous elements of the conquered society driven into them. In cases where they can safely be used for forced labour that may be done; but it must be recalled that the only good Jew is a dead Jew.' To aid him in his 'house cleaning' Heydrich brought in Odilo Globocnik who, for his part in the Trojan Horse operation in Czechoslovakia had been raised to the status of Gauleiter of Vienna but who, Heydrich cynically pointed out, 'was worthy of better things'. The 'better things' included a partnership with Eichmann which handled the 'resettlement' of hundreds of thousands of Jews in the record time of eight weeks. Murder squads of SS men carried out daily execution parades at which the previous day's captures by the Gestapo were marched into public squares, fields, barns or any other convenient venue and mown down with machine guns. The army generals protested against the atrocities they witnessed daily, but their protests only brought from Hitler warnings that if they interfered with Heydrich's designs ('which have my approval and authority') they might themselves strike trouble.

Within days of the forming of the Eichmann-Globocnik partnership a reign of terror had made nonsense of all attempts at formal government. A Polish peasant could be mutilated – castration was the favourite form – for being found on the streets ten minutes after curfew, his family arrested and dispersed to different concentration camps; many farmers were beaten to death for showing the slightest reluctance to provide whatever was demanded of them, even though it might leave them destitute; priests were shot for administering the Last Rites. The formal government – at the head of which Hitler had placed Hans Frank (no kin to the one-eyed Karl Frank who was to serve as Heydrich's chief of police in Prague), a battered old Nazi from Munich, and Seyss-Inquart, whose greatest success had been in the Fifth Column government of Austria – saw to it that all trials, legal or military, were suspended. As Heydrich reminded them, ultimate authority now rested with the RSHA or individually with its component parts the Gestapo and SD and no kind of proof was necessary when dealing with any suspected 'crime against the Reich'. So crimes against the Reich could be determined by any Gestapo thug who needed an outlet for his personal strain of sadism.

Throughout the winter of 1939–1940 Heydrich remained a bored and frustrated administrator of the instruments of terror in Poland. He had guided matters to that pass and now he sought new outlets. His sorties with the Luftwaffe gave him a certain amount of personal satisfaction; but neither the personal indulgence in dangerous activity in the air (for which he was many times reproached by Hitler) nor the accomplishment of RSHA power gave him full satisfaction. His interest was aroused when Hitler declared that the thirty million Slavs in the world were as great a threat as the Jews to the purity of the Germanic peoples and that they 'would have to be dealt with'; but Dunkirk, the planned invasion of Britain, and the Norwegian campaign were occupying the Führer's attention in the spring and summer of 1940, and the only mildly interesting thing

Artillery crosses the Polish frontier

Heydrich was ordered to do was to compile a 'black list' of names of people meriting special attention when the invasion operation Sea Lion was completed. (They included, naturally, Churchill and Harold Macmillan; but rather more mysteriously the novelist Rosita Forbes and the Church Lads' Brigade in its entirety.)

His interest flared somewhat more brightly when the so-called 'Madagascar plan' was resuscitated. This was an old notion for shovelling all the Jews in the world on to the French colony in the Indian Ocean, and with the fall of France it appeared to become a practical possibility. For Heydrich it seemed to offer an extension of his own political power, for as head of RSHA he would surely be appointed Hitler's envoy. But the plan came to nothing – for three reasons: first, because Britain, awake at last, did not capitulate after Dunkirk; secondly, because the 'Sea Lion' invasion was abandoned after the RAF's proved

Polish Jews are set to dig their own graves

resistance in the Battle of Britain and Hitler's decision to spread the war to the eastern front; and thirdly because the seizure of Madagascar would have prejudiced the settlement with the Vichy government of France.

Heydrich's immediate hopes of achieving power subordinate only to that of the Führer, in a realm of his own, were thus dashed; but he had not forgotten that Bohemia-Moravia was in the charge of the incompetent and ailing Neurath and that had not greater things trembled on the brink of possibility he would by now have been appointed Protector.

He need not have been – and probably wasn't – apprehensive. He was well aware that Hitler had the highest regard for him. Also, he had plenty to occupy his mind. On 31st July 1941 he received the order to complete his solution to the problem of the Jews:

'In order to complete the mission imposed on you in the order of 24th January 1939, to solve the problem of the Jews by means of emigration or evacuation in the most suitable way in the circumstances leading to a possible solution; I herewith instruct you to make all the necessary organizational, practical and material preparations for a comprehensive solution of the Jewish question within the German area of influence in Europe.

'In so far as other central authorities are concerned they are to co-operate with you.

'I hereby instruct you further to submit to me as soon as possible a general plan with respect to organizational, practical and material means necessary – for the execution of the desired Final Solution of the Jewish question.'

That was the imprimatur. (Actually it was signed by Göring, who called himself, among other things, Commissioner for Jewish Affairs.) Having received it he set about finding the practical means for its implementation. The general plan as submitted was the responsibility of Himmler, who as *Reichsführer-SS* had administrative charge of the concentration camps, and it provided for a particular camp at Auschwitz being fitted out with gas chambers as the most expeditious method of 'evacuating' the Jews; but it was Heydrich who fed the camp with victims. His Gestapo and SD formations, now backed by the exigencies of war, could justify unlimited ruthlessness. As practical means to

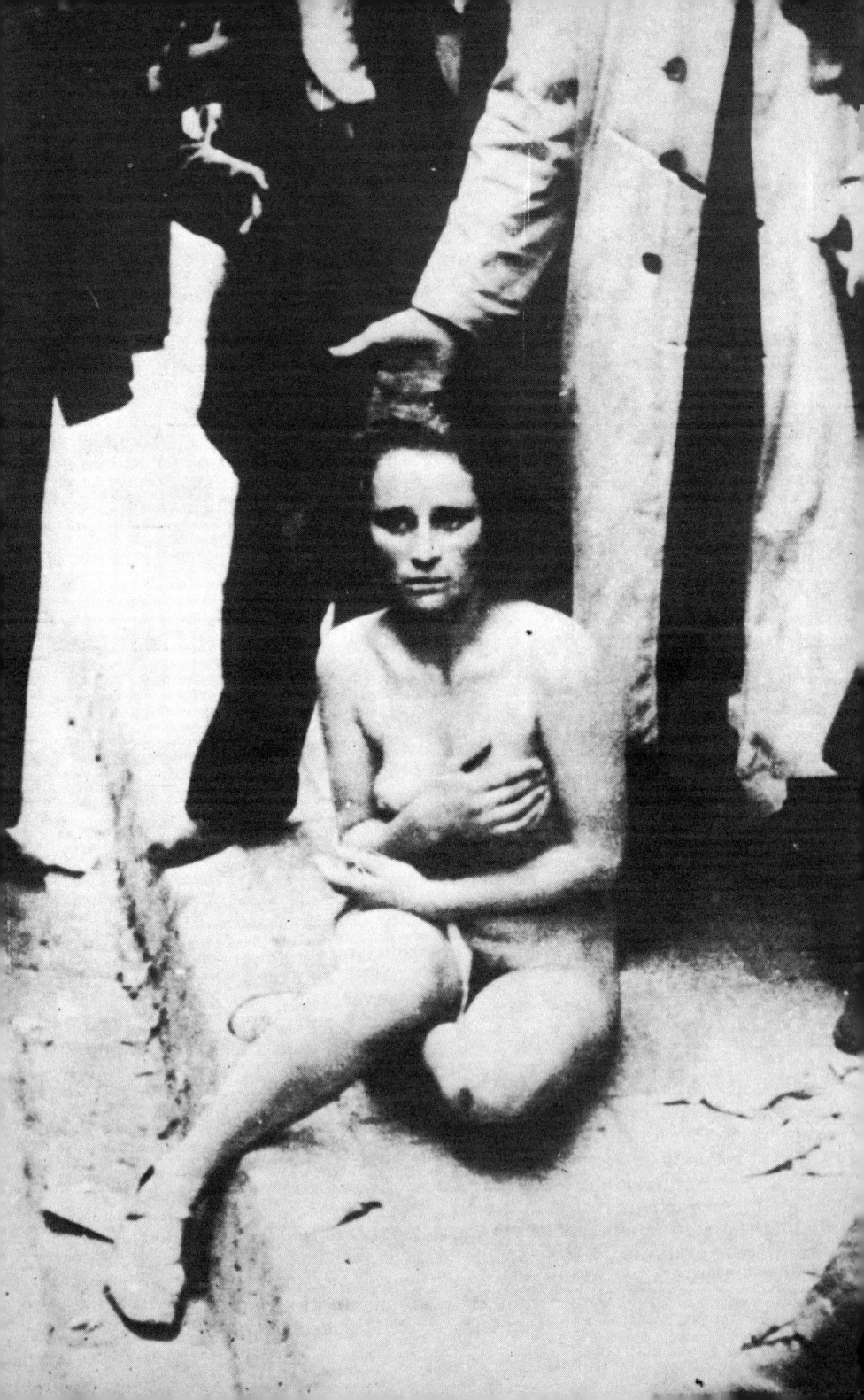

implement the plan they couldn't be bettered. The laden trains rolled across Germany daily carrying their wretched cargo, to be met at Auschwitz by Eichmann and his staff who, according to mood and circumstance, either dallied with each new intake by refreshing their hopes with promises of release after they had had baths and meals and their papers checked, or had them led under guard of SS men direct to the gas chambers into which they were thrust in orderly groups of ten as the guards called monotonously 'Zen! Zen! Zen!' At similar monotonous intervals the choked bodies were pulled from the exits and transported in trucks hauled by prisoners to the incinerators, from which the smoke rose in a black plume by night and day.

For three months Heydrich directed this dreadful traffic of death. In the few spare hours he was able to pluck from each week he joined Frau Canaris and her friends in chamber music of 'superlative quality'. (The description is Canaris's.) And his letters to his wife Lina suggest that at this time he was getting a great deal of pleasure from both his few off-duty hours and the work that was 'contributing fast to the solution we are all seeking to the racial problem'. Also, he was filled with hope that he would be 'free of the *Reichsführer-SS* and his crazy ideas shortly'.

In fact he was. In mid-September Hitler decided that the time had come to appoint his protégé to a position of real importance. 'The destruction of Jews is all very well, but it doesn't give a man a chance to stretch his abilities', he remarks in one of his interminable Table Talk dialogues. The destruction of Jews could in any case safely be left in the hands of Eichmann and his cronies, who continued to perform the task with exemplary promptitude until they had decimated the race by more than six million. The 'direction' of the Final

Pogrom in Lemberg, 1942

Rosita Forbes

Solution remained Heydrich's throughout the rest of his life, as the implementation remained Himmler's and the sordid details Eichmann's. It was a mechanically sound organization that mass-produced death with Teutonic efficiency – making sure even that the graves that were dug by the victims earmarked for the next 'Zen! Zen!' were economically filled by the bodies (they could in fact scarcely be called bodies, so cruelly tortured and emaciated were they) of their immediate predecessors; *id est*, should a particular grave seem in the guards' view to allow room for more Jewish flesh and bone after proper trampling down of the present contents, then the next decad would be crammed in. Efficiency demanded that there should be no wasted space. But though the direction remained Heydrich's it became, now, something of a spare-time operation; for on 27th September he wrote his bread-and-butter note to the Führer thanking him in the proper terms for his final triumph:

He111's on a bombing mission against London

'My Führer,

'I dutifully report that this afternoon, in accordance with today's Führer Decree, I took over the leadership of the affairs of Reich Protector of Bohemia-Moravia. The official takeover follows tomorrow at eleven in the morning, with the ceremony at Hradcany Castle.

'All political reports will reach you by the hand of Reichsleiter Bormann.

'Heil, mein Führer. And thank you for your confidence.

'Heydrich. *SS Obergruppenführer*.'

As Wighton says in his biography: 'As Hitler's Viceroy in the troubled Czech Protectorate of Bohemia-Moravia he now enjoyed the rank and privileges of a Minister of the Third Reich. And to signify the advance Himmler at last had that very morning granted him the rank of *Obergruppenführer* – his first SS promotion for seven years. He had gained rank, privileges, and the substantial financial advantages of which the miserly Himmler had always deprived him in the past . . . At last he was free of Himmler'.

He was not, however, and never would be, free of the terrible craving for power that was the heritage of his discovery of his tainted blood. As soon as he arrived in Prague with his chosen hangers-on he let it be known freely that he expected to be Hitler's successor. Hradcany Castle, to which he brought Lina and their children (there were now three – two boys and a girl) as soon as he took up residence, rang with the sound of wildly alcoholic parties at which he boasted of the Führer's wish to nominate him for that inglorious pinnacle of fame. His confidence in the assumption was not misplaced. Hitler had declared to confidantes that Heydrich had 'all the makings of a Führer of the Third Reich' and that he was taking steps to ensure the succession by decree. So far as is known he never did so; but that was no doubt because the neces-

Left: A Messerschmidt downed in southern England, 1940
Above: A German bomber falls victim in the Battle of Britain

sity was overtaken by Heydrich's assassination.

Far more terrible than any boastful assumptions of power, however, was the wave of despotic violence Heydrich set in motion as soon as he took over the reins.

Neurath had been sent on permanent sick leave to leave the Protector's chair vacant for the new incumbent. The Prime Minister, Alois Elias, was arrested and brought before a military court to answer charges of treason. Proof of his association with the exiled President, Beneš (who by now had made his headquarters in London and from there was directing the Czech underground resistance movement), had been provided by the Gestapo – and in this particular case had been provided without recourse to trickery, for there was no doubt that Elias was sympathetic to the Resistance and had been careless enough to leave clues to the association where they could be picked up by *leute* and pieced together by the SD. A confession was wrung from him ('H[eydrich] phoned to say Elias had confessed', Himmler wrote in his diary) and he was shot four days after his arrest. The President, Dr Hacha, Benes' successor, had to be treated differently – not because he was senile and useless (which he was) but because he had turned from suspicious neutrality to pro-Nazism and was looked on by Hitler with what passed for benevolence. Neither Prime Minister nor President formed the slightest threat to the absolute power of the Protector; they were there only to back the illusion that the Czechs had been left with the figureheads of a democratic government; but having exemplarily removed Elias, Heydrich summoned the Government and warned them that things would be run differently now that he had taken over the reins from Neurath. The transcript of his speech was produced at the Nuremberg trials. It said, in part:

'It is time you realized that the day of parliamentary ministerial decisions, which only hinder the practical measures of government and the work of leadership, has gone. The smaller the ministry the more successful will be the achievement. Get out of your heads that you can continue the tricks of the democratic party politicians. The first principle of our work together must be mutual confidence.' He then, naturally, purged the government (which anyway was scarcely more than a bureaucratic machine for administration) of elements alien to Nazi doctrine and announced a programme of 're-education to clarify and correct errors in the teaching of Czech youth'. To this he added the ominous words 'Accounts with the Czech Resistance movement will also be settled'.

The 're-education' and 'settlement of debts' followed the usual Nazi pattern of arrests, deportation to the concentration camps, and murder. For nine months a wave of terror submerged the Protectorate. Its miseries were alleviated only by the granting to 'the workers' of increased rations; but the chosen workers were specifically those at the Skoda armaments works and the increase had no other motive than the maintenance of supplies for the German war effort. 'Intellectuals' – who included teachers, the priesthood, writers and anyone else who by words or actions had the potential power of influencing thought – were rounded up, interrogated and dealt with summarily by day and night. The murder squads practised their deadly duty daily in the courtyard of Hradcany Castle while Heydrich watched from the window of the tapestry-hung office he had appropriated as suitable for his status; the slatted cattle trucks stood at the loading bays of the railway station awaiting their cargo for the concentration camps and the gas chambers. But this engulfing wave of

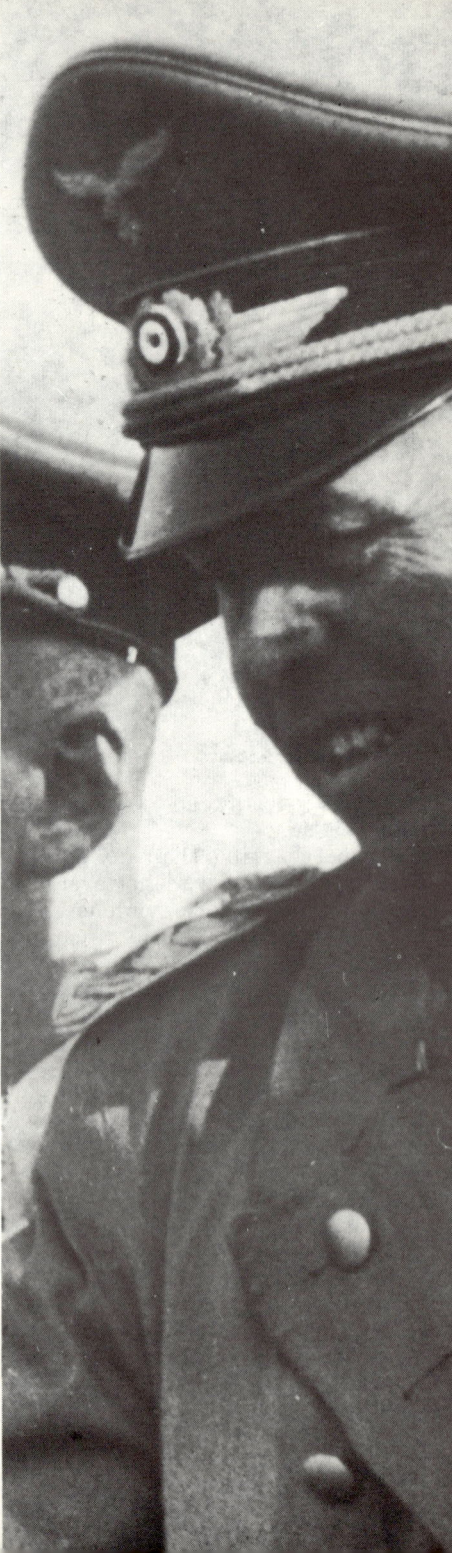

Field-Marshal Kesselring with Goring

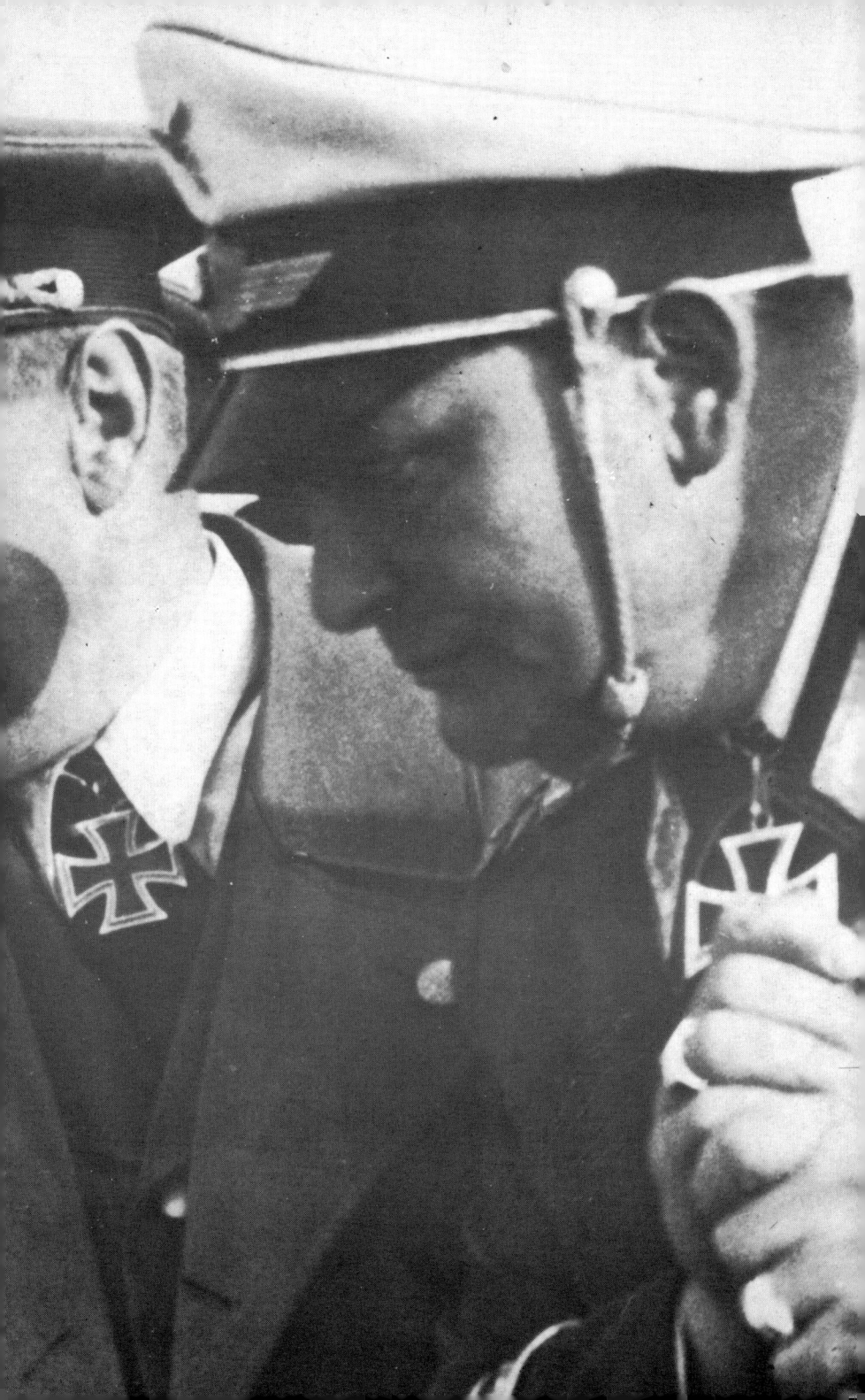

Left: Rollcall in Sachsenhausen, winter 1941. *Above:* Hradcany Castle, Prague

violence and terror was meant to deal only with the immediate situation – as Heydrich put it, 'The threat of dagger-blows to the Reich in the form of sabotage, go - slow movements among the workers, terror-group activities, all organized by what is obviously a large-scale Resistance movement'. A far more embracing plan of extermination was already in Heydrich's desk in the form of a secret order from Hitler. It was nothing less than the first step to be taken toward another Final Solution – a far greater one than even that of the Jews: the extermination of the entire Slav peoples, of whom Himmler's special bureau dealing with ideologies and racial statistics had pronounced the existence of thirty millions.

'I have accepted your plan for destroying the Czech nation', Hitler wrote. 'Basically it will cover three points: the Germanization of as great a proportion of the Czechs as possible; the deportation or extermination of those Czechs who cannot be absorbed and of the intelligentsia hostile to the

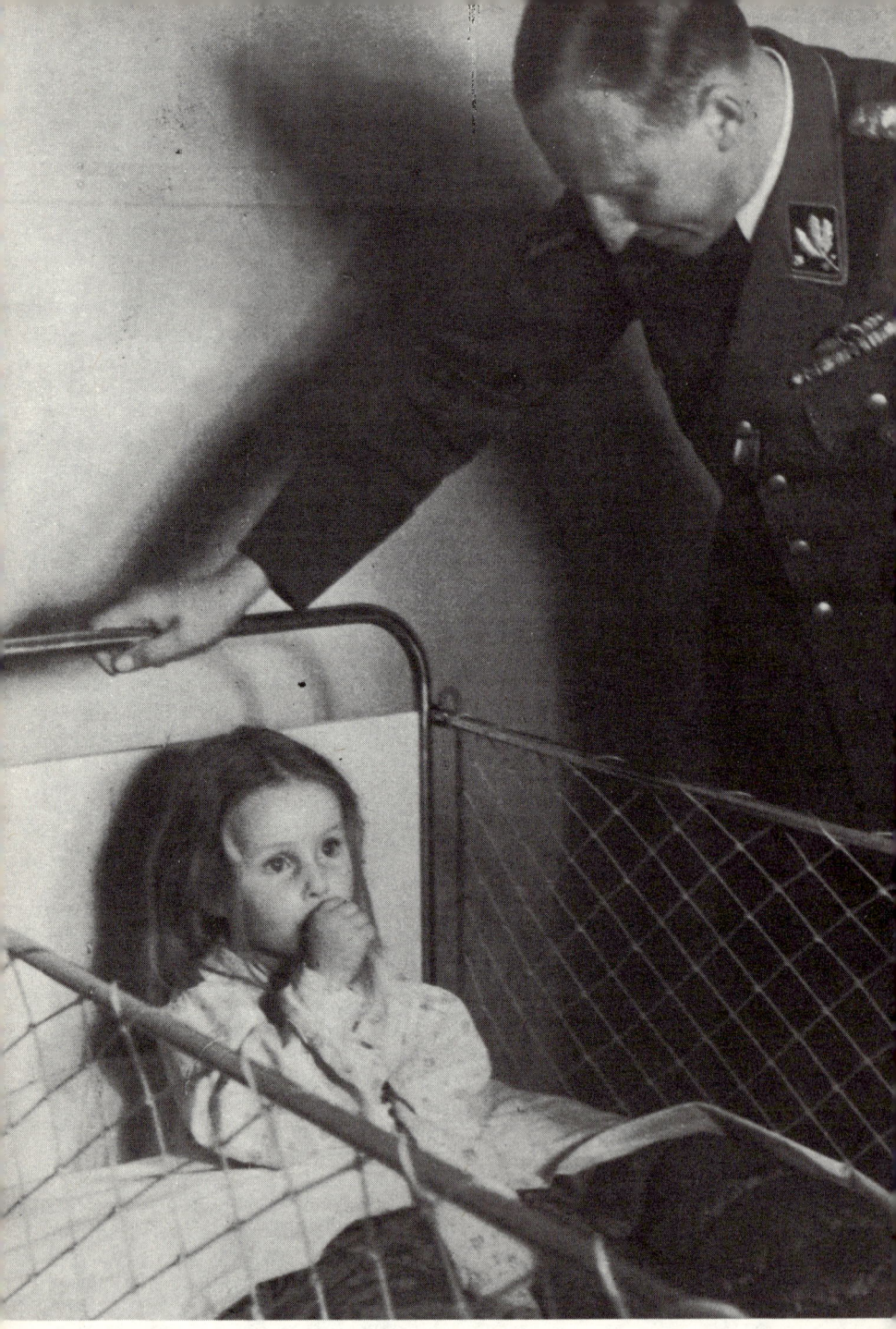

Above: Heydrich, the family man, bids goodnight to his eldest daughter.
Right: Dr Hacha

Reich; and resettlement of the space freed by these measures with good German blood. To that basis I add my decree: that Czechs about whom there exists doubt from the racial standpoint – or who are antagonistic toward the Reich – must be excluded from assimilation. *This category must be exterminated.*'

It was toward the furtherance of this scheme of extermination that Heydrich directed all his energies during the first months of his office. And it was with a portfolio of plans for 'the resettlement of those whose worth has been proved by every means at my command' that he set out for Berlin on the morning of Wednesday 27th May 1942.

The night before he had attended a concert given by old pupils of his father. It had pleased him and he had telephoned Halle-on-Saale to say so. 'Just what I needed', he told his father, 'to relieve the cares of office. I shall be flying to Berlin in the morning to see the Führer. The music put me in the right mood'.

He was still in a good mood as he played with his children in the garden of his house in Jungfern-Breschen. Had he been going to his office in Prague he would have had to leave earlier, but his plane would not be ready for takeoff before eleven o'clock. It was a fine spring morning with the mist rising from the valley of the Vltava and he lingered as long as he could. But shortly after ten he summoned his chauffeur, Klein, who said later that he was humming cheerfully as he got into the Mercedes, set his briefcase on his lap, took out a thick wodge of papers, and settled himself to study them. There was a nice irony in the fact that they dealt with the matter of the extermination of the Slav peoples. At ten past ten the car started off on its journey down the hill toward the waiting assassins, and death.

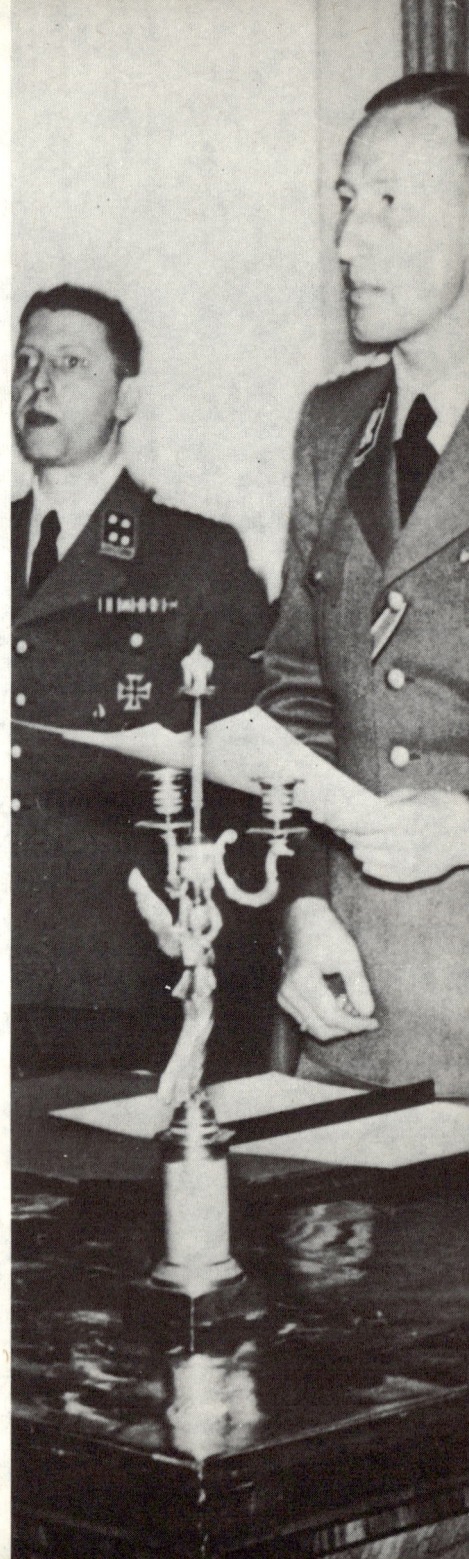

Heydrich, with Dr Frank, holds a press conference just before his assassination

Bibliography

The Rise and Fall of the Third Reich William L Shirer (London: Secker & Warburg)
SS: Alibi of a Nation Gerald Reitlinger (London: Heinemann)
The Waffen SS George Stein (New York: Cornell)
The Mind of Adolf Hitler Walter Langer (London: Secker & Warburg)
The Final Solution Gerald Reitlinger (London: Vallentine, Mitchell)
The Arms of Krupp William Manchester (London: Michael Joseph)
The Face of the Third Reich Joachim Fest (London: Weidenfeld & Nicolson)
The Nemesis of Power Sir John Wheeler-Bennett (London: Heinemann)
Hitler Alan Bullock (London: Odhams)
Heydrich Charles Wighton (London)
Memoirs Walter Schellenberg (London: Heinemann)

Don't miss Ballantine's best-selling, standard-size War Books—many with photographs—$1.25 each:

SUICIDE SUBMARINE!
Yutaka Yokota with Joseph D. Harrington

BRAZEN CHARIOTS
Major Robert Crisp

THE THOUSAND-MILE WAR
Brian Garfield

ZERO!
Masatake Okumiya and Jiro Horikoshi with Martin Caidin

THE BRIDGE AT REMAGEN
Ken Hechler

THE MIDGET RAIDERS
C.E.T. Warren and James Benson

CURRAHEE!
Donald R. Burgett

THE FIRST AND THE LAST
Adolf Galland

STUKA PILOT
Hans Ulrich Rudel

U-BOATS AT WAR
Harald Busch

THUNDERBOLT!
Robert S. Johnson with Martin Caidin

DECISION AT ST.-VITH
Charles Whiting

WING LEADER
Group Captain J. E. Johnson

GUERRILLA SUBMARINES
Edward Dissette and H. C. Adamson

THE DESTRUCTION OF DRESDEN
David Irving

To order by mail, send price of book plus 25¢ per order for handling to Ballantine Cash Sales, P.O. Box 505, Westminster, Maryland 21157. Please allow three weeks for delivery.